THE THAMES & SEVERN CANAL

THROUGH TIME

David Viner

AMBERLEY PUBLISHING

Dedicated to the memory of Humphrey Household (1906–1996),
whose book first inspired my interest in the history and surviving heritage
of the Thames & Severn Canal

About the Author

David Viner was Curator of the Corinium Museum in Cirencester 1971–98, and is a freelance curator, independent researcher and writer. This is his fourth book on the Thames & Severn Canal.

Further Reading

Cuss, Edwin and Mills, Mike, *The Stroudwater and Thames & Severn Canals From Old Photographs* (Vol. 1 1988 and 2012; Vol. 2 1993 and 2010; Vol. 3 2013)
Handford, Michael and Viner, David, *Stroudwater & Thames & Severn Canals Towpath Guide* (1984 & 1988)
Handford, Michael, *The Cotswold Canals Towpath Guide: The Stroudwater Navigation* (2012)
Household, Humphrey, *The Thames & Severn Canal* (1969, 1983 & 2009)
Tucker, Joan, *The Stroudwater Navigation: A Social History* (2003)
Viner, David, *The Thames & Seven Canal: A Survey from Historical Photographs* (1975)
Viner, David, *The Thames & Severn Canal: History & Guide* (2002)

A Note on Access

Many canal-side properties remain private, and reference to building, land and property in these pages does not imply any right of access.

First published 2013

Amberley Publishing
The Hill, Stroud
Gloucestershire, GL5 4EP

www.amberley-books.com

Copyright © David Viner, 2013

The right of David Viner to be identified as the
Author of this work has been asserted in accordance
with the Copyrights, Designs and Patents Act 1988.

ISBN 978 1 84868 044 9

British Library Cataloguing in Publication Data.
A catalogue record for this book is available from
the British Library.

Typeset in 9.5pt on 12pt Celeste.
Typesetting by Amberley Publishing.
Printed in the UK.

Introduction

Nostalgia is a wonderful thing, it is said, and it has certainly buoyed up much public feeling about neglected parts of our historic transport system, canals and railways in particular. The sight of a derelict canal and its associated buildings can bring forth feelings of frustration at an opportunity lost (or even deliberately neglected), leading to a bandwagon of restoration activity over the past half-century or more. But such dereliction can also encourage a vast range of nature conservation and wider environmental opportunities, especially in such a wonderful landscape as the Cotswold Hills and delightful hidden river valleys. The real challenge is finding a true balance between these apparently conflicting interests.

Today, a visitor to the historic line of the Thames & Severn Canal, over eighty years after the last working or commercial boat disturbed its waters, can see at first-hand the progress being made on all these fronts and can also enjoy a rich mixture of old and new. Around half of the towpath along the 30-mile length of the canal between the centre of Stroud and Inglesham has already been maintained or restored to public use. This is one of the four principal aims of the Cotswold Canals Trust, to provide a backbone for access and enjoyment. It is to be hoped that more may be added in future, respecting the original line.

The Thames & Severn Canal opened in 1789. It was the fulfilment of one of the earliest of many proposals to link British river navigations across a watershed, in this case between the two great rivers of southern Britain. The canal took five years to build and at Sapperton boasted the longest and largest canal tunnel in the world at the time. From its junction with the Stroudwater Navigation in Stroud (from where it linked directly into the River Severn at Framilode), the Thames & Severn ran up the Golden Valley and across the Cotswolds and so via the upper reaches of the infant Thames joined that great river at

Inglesham near Lechlade. After a century or more of commercial use, much of it essentially local rather than through-route as the original plan intended, its decline seriously set in and the official and final closure dates of 1927 and 1933 tell their own story.

This album presents images old and new, grouped to reflect changes over time, not merely the same view contrasted each time to show 'then and now'. This has been made possible not least by the quite substantial accumulations of colour images taken over the past thirty or more years, and already of historic value, which it is hoped these pages reflect. For example, a number were taken in the summer of 1980. More recent scenes were taken during concentrated sessions on dates between 2006 and 2012, March to May being a favourite period for exploration. Of the earlier period images, there is a strong emphasis on the canal's built heritage, an outstanding legacy that frames the entire story of the Thames & Severn.

Where canal historian Humphrey Household's high-quality photographs have been available, a determined effort has been made to include them, so effective are they in capturing the mood along the canal in the post-Second World War years, the traffic having gone and an uncertain future ahead.

Household's work has been much admired (not least by the author of this album), but he was no sentimentalist dreaming of a lost past. His was a record of endeavour, diligently studied over many years in the considerable body of surviving T&S archives; for him future restoration was an uncertain business altogether. On this last point he was not alone. Two of the twentieth-century's principal canal historians and writers also had their say about significance and potential, words that ring down the decades as both a warning and a stimulus to present and future restoration campaigns.

Tom Rolt in his delightful *Narrow Boat* (1944) described the Thames & Severn and its loss as 'most beautiful and tragic of all', its route 'climbing up the Golden Valley between great hills that wear their beechwoods like a mane'. He deeply regretted its passing. In later years, Charles Hadfield, distinguished author of a large number of canal histories, expressed similar regret while welcoming Household's book into the world in 1969. He thought the journey by water along the length of this particular canal close to his own home 'would have been joy indeed', so attractive was the countryside through which it passed and so great the achievement of its construction. It is hoped that something of such feelings may be stirred from among the photographs presented here in this album.

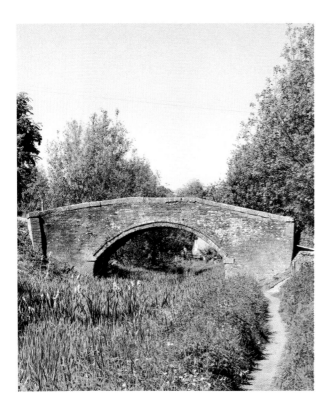

The Thames & Severn Canal

In addition to the spectacular scenery through which it passes, the canal is equally impressive in its statistics. From Stroud, it rises 241 feet to the summit level and thereafter descends 129 feet to the Thames. Over 30 miles, it has forty-four locks, twenty-eight on the ascent and sixteen on the descent. Climbing to the summit at Daneway there are twelve locks in little more than 1½ miles, with seven in the final half mile to the top. All this is impressive enough before the long journey through the 2¼-mile-long Sapperton tunnel. Five round houses are particularly noteworthy features. The map shows the entire length, including the 7-mile Stroudwater Canal, and includes the planned phases of restoration of which 1A is in active progress, with sections of phase 2 being pursued in parallel. On the Thames & Severn, the accessible towpath sections are Stroud to Daneway, and Siddington to Latton, with a shorter delightful section from Coates to Thames Head.

Above is a view of Stanton's Bridge, a symbol of utility with elegance and a classic Thames & Severn Canal bridge.

(*Map courtesy of Cotswold Canals Trust*)

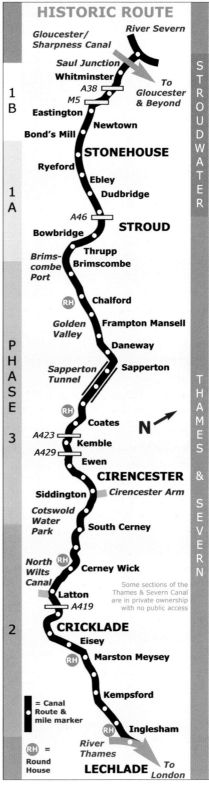

HISTORIC ROUTE

River Severn
Gloucester/Sharpness Canal
Saul Junction
Whitminster
A38
M5
To Gloucester & Beyond
Eastington
Newtown
Bond's Mill
STONEHOUSE
Ryeford
Ebley
Dudbridge
A46
STROUD
Bowbridge
Thrupp
Brimscombe Port
Brimscombe
RH Chalford
Golden Valley
Frampton Mansell
Daneway
Sapperton Tunnel
Sapperton
RH
Coates
A423
Kemble
A429
Ewen
CIRENCESTER
Siddington
Cirencester Arm
Cotswold Water Park
South Cerney
North Wilts Canal
RH Cerney Wick

Some sections of the Thames & Severn Canal are in private ownership with no public access

Latton
A419
CRICKLADE
Eisey
RH Marston Meysey
Kempsford
= Canal Route & mile marker
RH Inglesham
River Thames
RH = Round House
LECHLADE
To London

N

PHASE 3
PHASE 2
1 B
1 A

STROUDWATER
THAMES & SEVERN

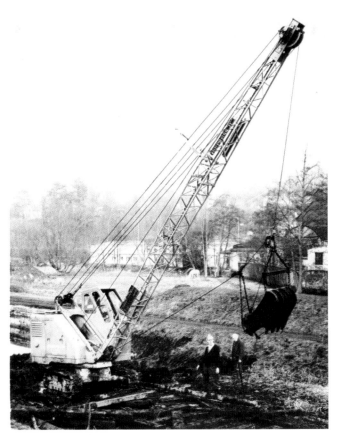

Restoring the Thames & Severn Canal

The restoration campaign really began with the formation of the Stroudwater Canal Society (now Cotswold Canals Trust) in 1972. Its early campaigns included its first worksite, above Bowbridge, dredging and re-flooding the ¾-mile pound up to Griffin's Mill Lock using a Priestman excavator. Some forty years on, in February 2012, the latest high-profile achievement was the restoration of the whole Wallbridge area in Stroud, celebrated with a visit by HRH The Princess Royal to Wallbridge Upper Lock and a boat trip to view the new road bridge, with an appreciative if cold crowd of supporters on a snowy day.

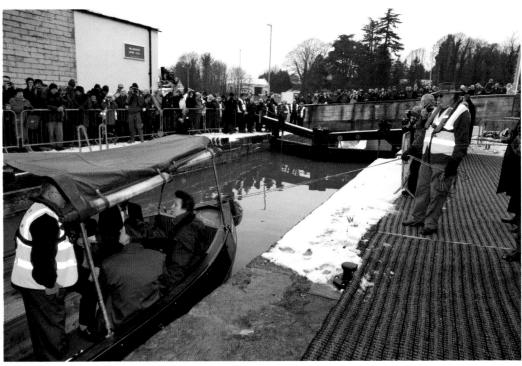

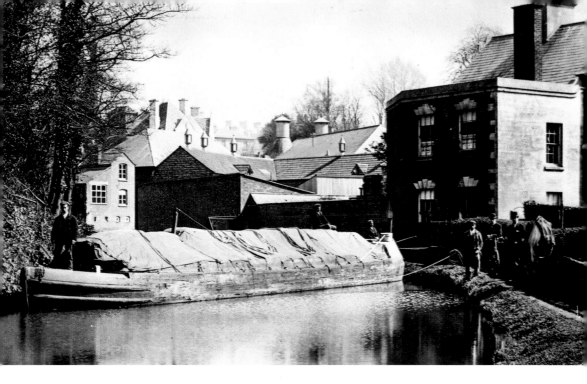

Wallbridge

The Thames & Severn begins at Wallbridge Lower Lock, passing between former Stroud Brewery buildings to reach Upper Lock. A memorable event recorded here on 11 April 1899 celebrated a reopening of the through canal line. The longboat *Trial* is returning to Stonehouse from London with a cargo of wool for Charles Hooper & Sons, mill owners of Eastington, a round trip of three weeks. On 14 May 1980 the Wallbridge area looks quite different, bereft of the old brewery buildings but with the Stroudwater Company's headquarters building intact, seen here from the rear.

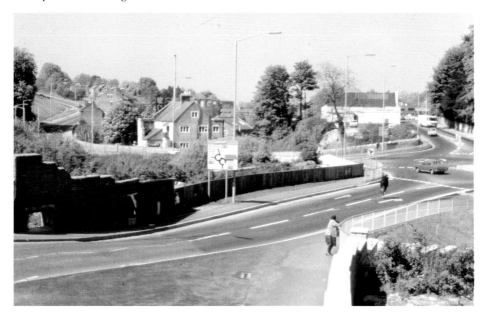

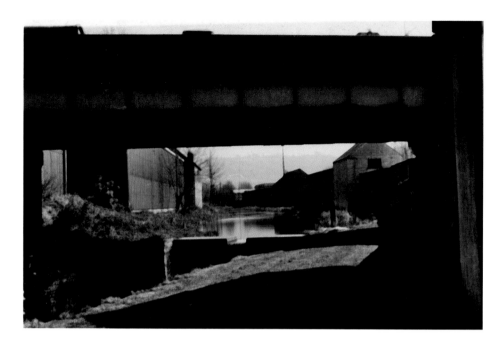

Wallbridge

A bleak view of the Upper Lock is framed by the overbridge of the former Midland Railway, built in 1885/86 to give access from Stroud town centre into its station and yard, and is a constant reminder of railway competition for the canal's business. The lock remains derelict and gateless, with a dam in place. By March 2012 this whole area had been transformed, with the lock re-gated and useable, and a café plying for trade alongside. Over the towpath wall, some earlier buildings survive on the railway site.

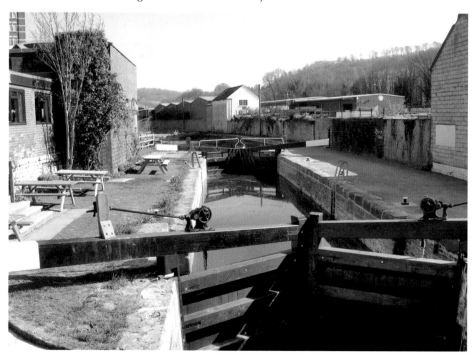

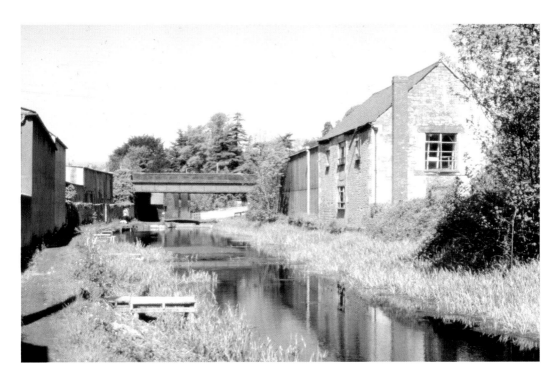

Wallbridge Wharf

The railway bridge over the lock remains a feature on 14 May 1980, but the canal holds a good supply of water used by the local fishing club. The Thames & Severn Company's own wharf, not to be confused with the Stroudwater's competing wharf nearby, stands on the north side, built in 1828 to handle an expansion of business. By May 2009, wharf building and site were derelict, with some of the previously-impressive stone retaining wall demolished. Hill, Paul & Co.'s former clothing factory of 1898 stands behind, now restored.

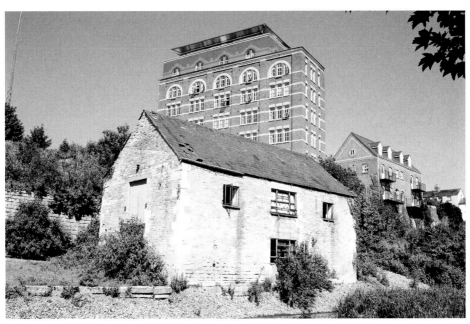

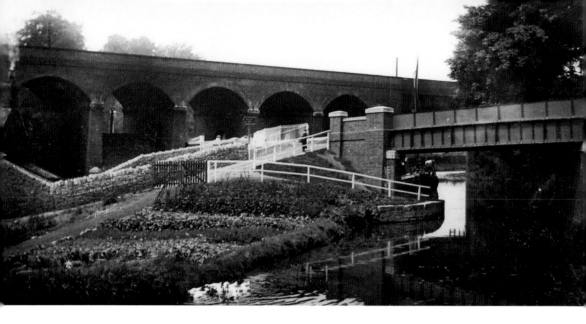

Under the Railway to Capel's Mill

Latest developments for the canal's restoration are at Capel's Mill, where a new line is being created through a section that has long been infilled. Two railway companies dominated this scene, the GWR viaduct of 1844 in the background taking much of the mill site and the later Midland Railway bridge leading up to its carriers' stables. This view from around 1910 shows how the towpath crosses sides; a barge or trow lies just beyond. In March 2013 the new cut is taking shape, the imposition of modern civil engineering skills upon a much altered landscape.

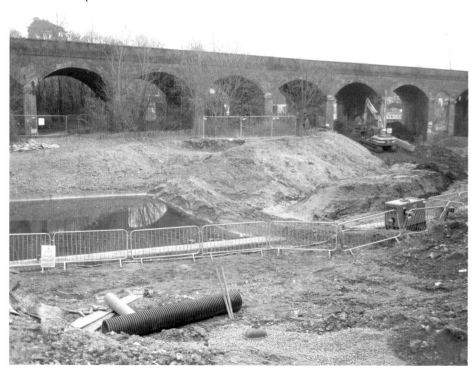

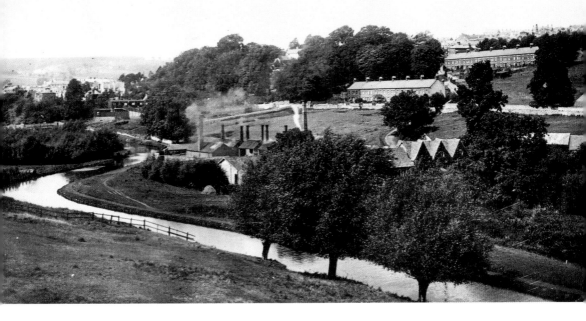

Arundel's Towpath

Beyond Capel's is a sense of the quiet valley floor, and previous industrial history seems almost to have vanished. Avoided by the canal, Arundel's Mill has disappeared; the only indications of its existence are the dredged millpond and sluices. New housing now stands on the site. Many mills were named after one of the principal owners in their history; Richard Arundel owned this mill in the early seventeenth century. It was also typical for the many variations in its production, usually based upon the processing of wool, with a dyeing business as its last use.

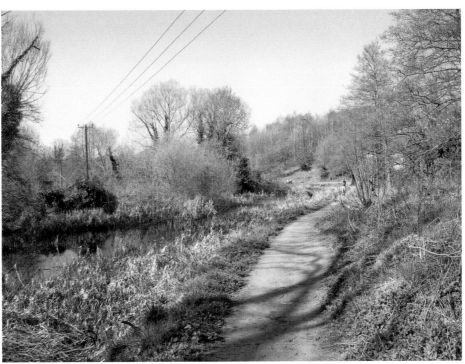

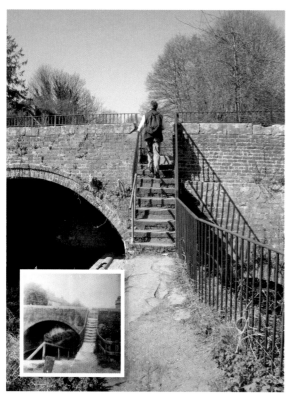

Bowbridge Lock

Approaching Bowbridge the towpath becomes a well-worn, single-width path in the narrow confine between the River Frome and the canal, only yards apart here. Steps up either side lead onto the bridge, over which passes one of the many north–south packhorse and pedestrian routes crossing the valley before the turnpike road was built along the Frome Valley in 1814. Bowbridge is the site of the first real achievement in restoration by Cotswold Canals Trust in the 1970s, periodic maintenance being required thereafter to sustain the effort, as seen here in May 2009.

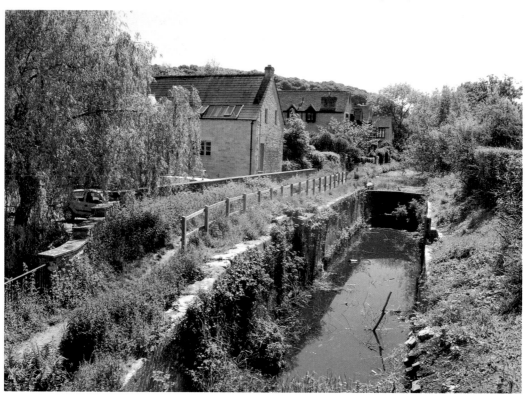

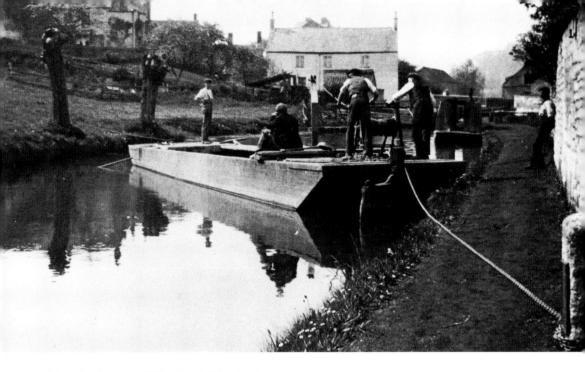

Temple Thurston Visits Bowbridge Lock

Photographs of working activity along the Thames & Severn are comparatively rare. These maintenance scenes were captured just above the lock at Bowbridge around 1911 by E. Temple Thurston while researching *The Flower of Gloster* – his evocative and invaluable record towards the end of the canal's working life. A spoon or scoop dredge is being used, formed of a leather bag on an iron ring at the end of a long pole, lowered over the side, dragged along the bottom and then raised by a windlass. The 1-mile milestone secures the boats.

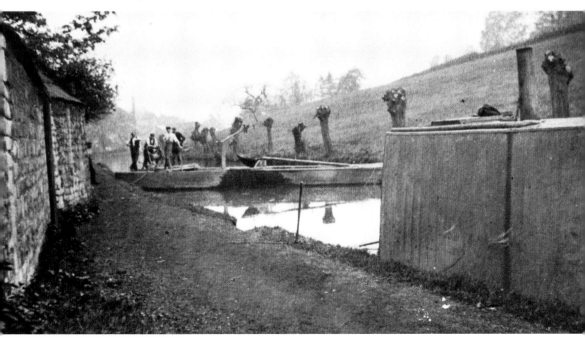

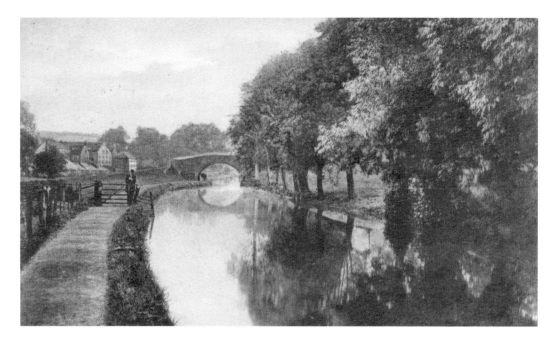

Stanton's Bridge

The view to Stanton's Bridge between Bowbridge and Griffin's Mill Locks depicts a classic canal scene, then and now. The Stanton family name is associated with woollen manufacturers in the Frome Valley, including nearby Stafford Mill. This bridge is the first encountered coming up from Stroud where the attractiveness of its simple shape and design can be fully appreciated as functional yet elegant. For many years, half of the parapet had been missing with some coping stones lying in the canal bed. Restored, the bridge was 'topped out' in December 1975.

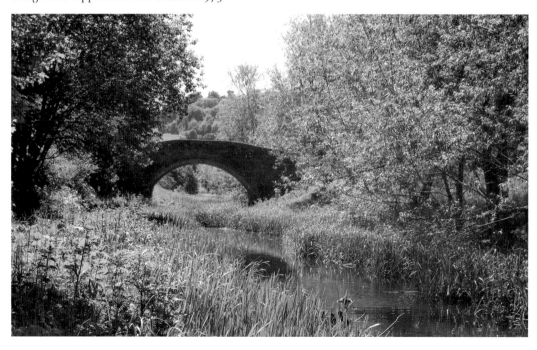

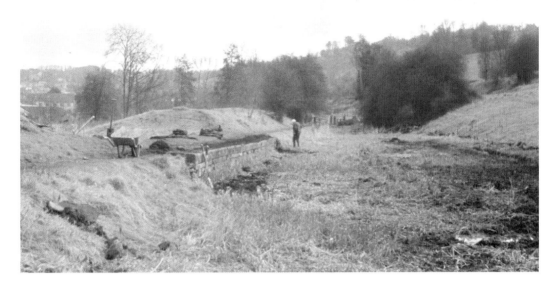

Griffin's Mill Lock

Restoration by dragline of this section of canal above Stanton's Bridge in the early 1970s also included exposure and cleaning up of this isolated stone wharf, surviving in good order and one of those small but fascinating parts of the canal's story. Did this wharf have a name? Griffin's Mill Lock just above was still derelict. When Henry Rodolph de Salis undertook his survey of the Thames & Severn in 1896, while studying the state of the canal system generally, he recorded the lock looking functional if rather rundown.

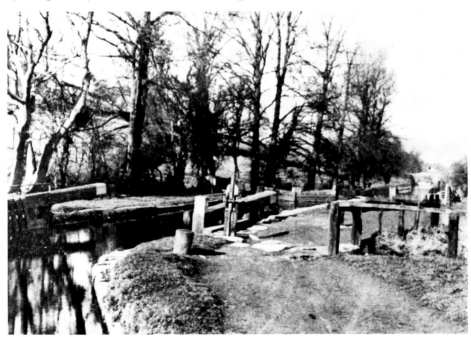

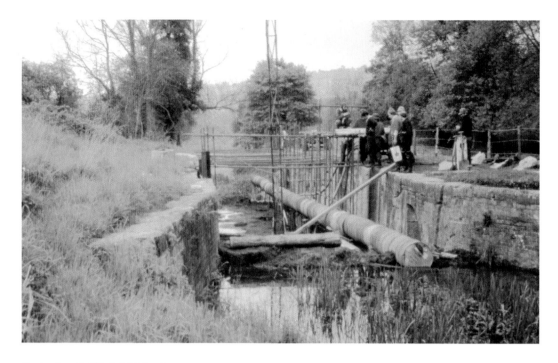

Restoring Griffin's Mill Lock

Shortage of funds plus native ingenuity lay behind a 150-foot-long oil drum 'pipeline' at Griffin's Mill Lock restored in the mid-1970s, its purpose to transfer water through the lock and facilitate the removal of tons of silt from the chamber. This project was also noteworthy for the manufacture of the first new lock gate in the campaign. The view towards Stanton's Bridge in May 1980 is a reminder of the challenge not only of replacing gates but repairing the stone and brickwork of the lock structure.

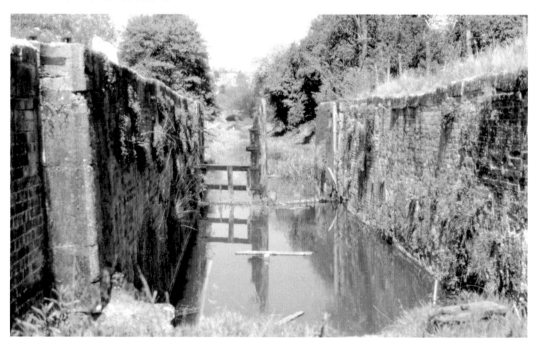

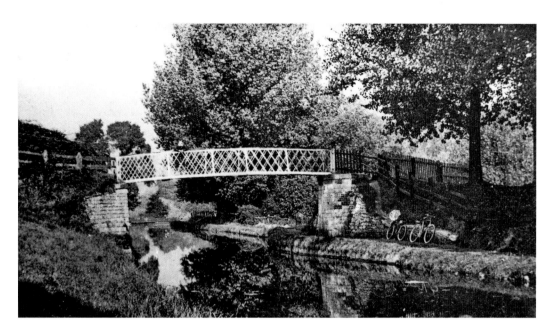

Jubilee Bridge to Ham Mill Lock

A delightful small iron lattice footbridge crosses the canal, serving the needs of the local community along the valley and providing workers' access to Griffin's Mill. Replacing earlier structures, its name and suggested date of 1903 are a reminder of late nineteenth-century celebrations for Queen Victoria in 1887 and 1897. In the spring sunshine of 2012, the dam and weir at Ham Mill Lock look serene, and the canal is well watered.

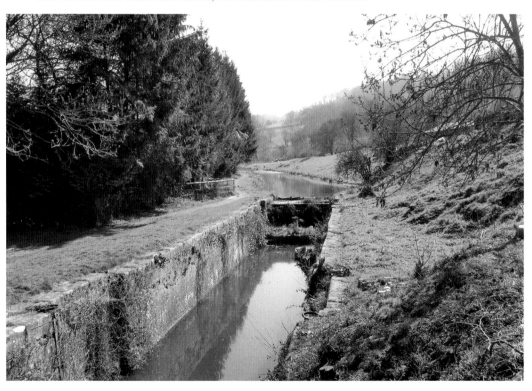

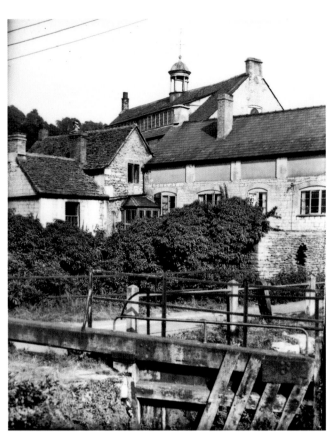

Hope Mill

Humphrey Household captured this view across the lock gates to Hope Mill in August 1947, an interesting mixture of buildings of various dates and uses, mostly linked to the processes in woollen cloth manufacture. Some buildings were demolished in the 1960s, the site becoming a caravan park and an industrial estate. By March 1985 the infilled line of lock and canal had to be searched for here, although one surviving mill building anchors the scene looking back towards Stroud.

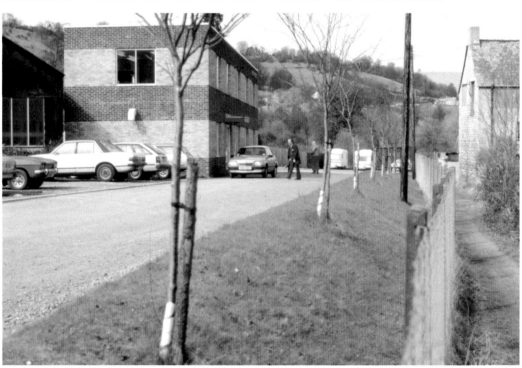

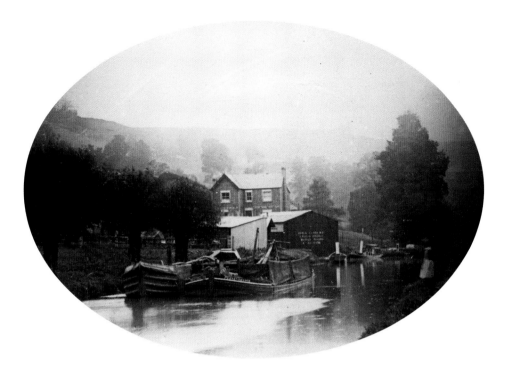

Building Canal & Riverboats at Hope Mill

Edwin Clark & Company operated a flourishing steamboat manufacturing business producing some fifty-five boats, nearly all in steel, at its canal ironworks for more than a decade until Clark's early death in 1896. In this view of around 1889, his home at Hope Villa stands beyond the boat sheds. The successor company was Abdela & Mitchell Ltd and *Humaytha* represents a very typical product. Designed and constructed in 1905 for use in Brazil, it had gross tonnage of 27 tons, and was 75 feet long with a 150 hp engine, ideal for South American or other colonial river systems.

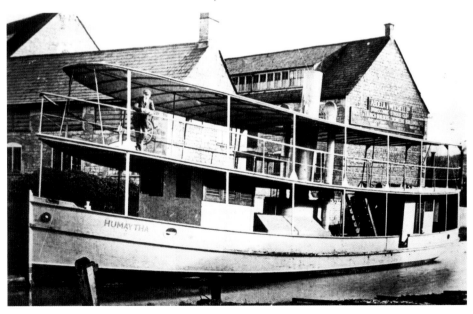

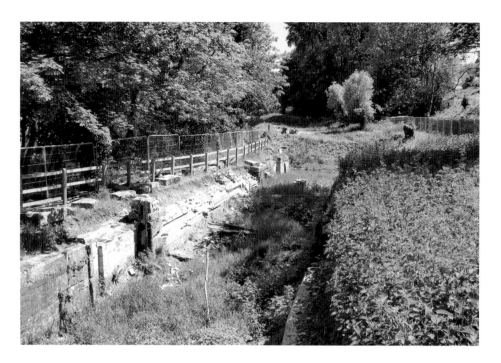

Gough's Orchard Lock

Two views, three years apart, between spring 2009 and 2012, at the charmingly-named Gough's Orchard Lock. As with all locks up to Bourne, the dimensions of 74 feet in length and 15 feet 6 inches wide reflect the wider barges and trows of the Severn river and canal system. Good progress with restoration of the lock chamber was achieved via energetic Waterway Recovery Group working parties and a £50,000 donation specific to this site. The humpbacked bridge is the fourth encountered coming up from Stroud so far.

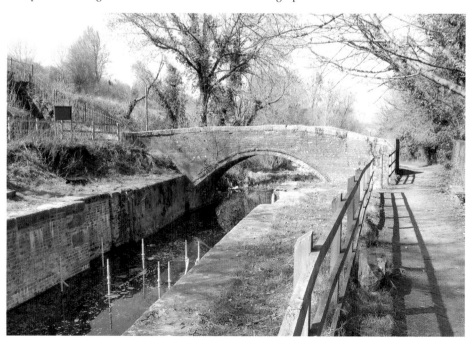

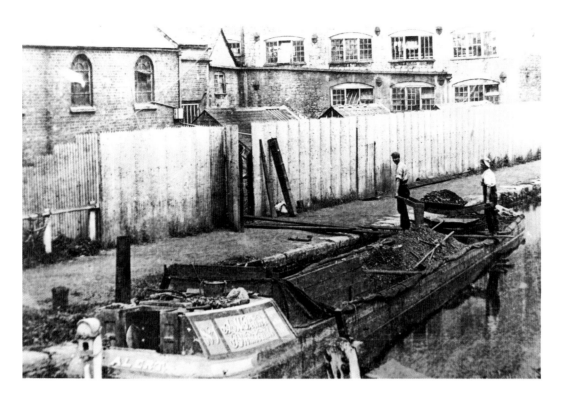

Brimscombe Mill & Bridge

A remarkable surviving scene of a working boat on the Thames & Severn; coal is being unloaded into Brimscombe Mills from the longboat *Alert*, owned by A. M. Pearce of Brimscombe, sometime between 1910 and 1930. The boat is moored by the stern to the top gates of Gough's Orchard Lock, with the coal unloaded straight into the mill by two (unrelated) men named Davis, of Chalford. Much of this site has now been cleared. Round the bend is the now levelled Brimscombe Bridge and the Ship Inn, happily still in business today.

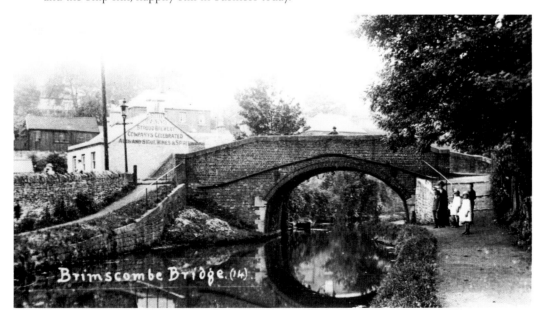

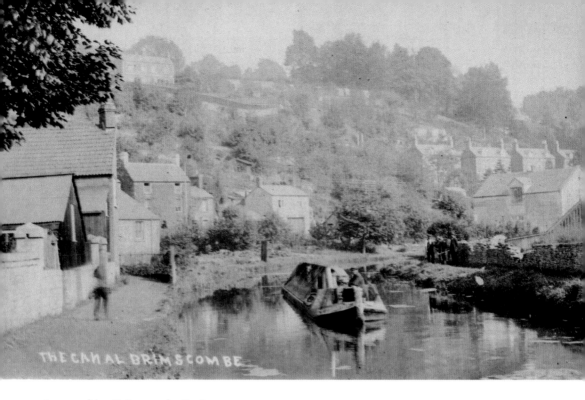

THE CANAL BRIMSCOMBE

Approaching Brimscombe Port

From the bridge the canal swings round into Brimscombe Port, the main building coming up on the right in this scene. There is a towpath on both banks, giving access to the north and south sides of the port. The horse-drawn longboat edges slowly round the bend in around 1915. In March 2012, the buildings on the left anchor the scene and the access road follows the canal line, but the remainder is now an industrial estate, still respecting the Brimscombe Port name.

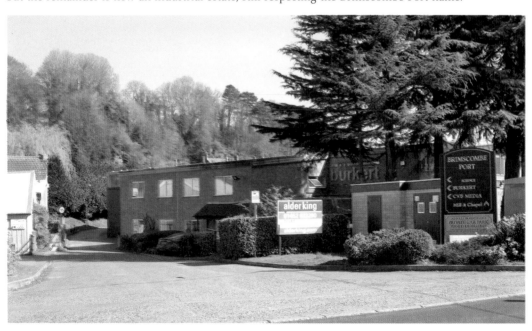

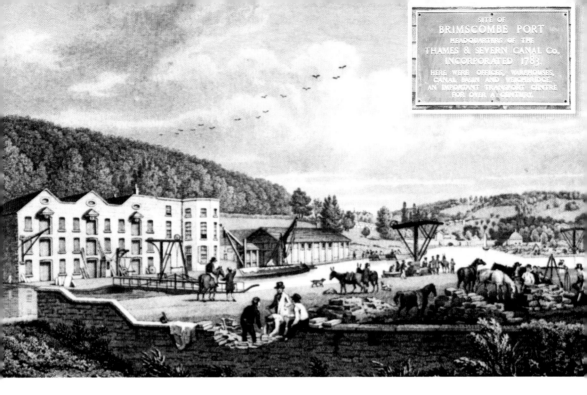

Brimscombe Port

Brimscombe Port was the focal point of the life of the Thames & Severn and its early headquarters, staffed with upwards of seventeen clerks, apprentices, wharfmen, labourers and craftsmen. Such activity can be appreciated in the 1826 illustration published in *Delineations of Gloucestershire* and the later view around 1910, looking east to Bourne Mill and bridge. Cranes, warehousing, the boat-weighing machine and other facilities await business. The port's significance was as an inland trans-shipment point between vessels of different gauges, principally the Severn trows and the western types of Thames barges.

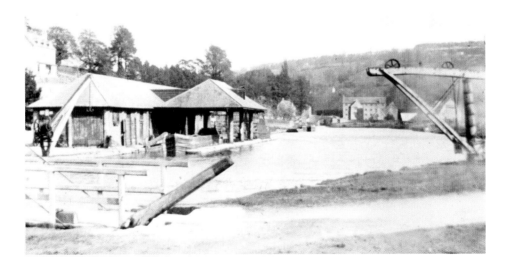

23

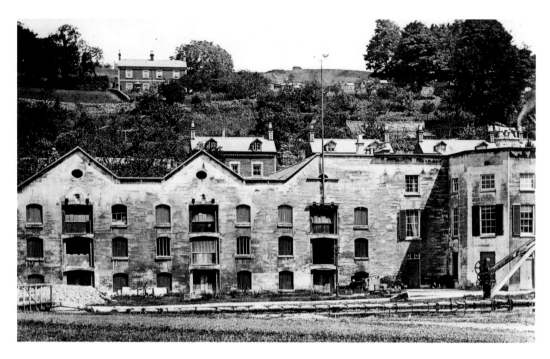

Brimscombe Port

The port was a large basin around 700 feet long and 250 feet wide, which it is said could hold 100 vessels. A central island was used for storing coal and other goods susceptible to theft. Along the northern side was the principal wharf with its main building, a remarkable structure containing a warehouse, an office and an agent's house over three storeys, recorded to have been built by master mason Thomas Cook from Painswick. Utilitarian factory buildings replaced all this in the 1960s, as seen here in May 1980 and still there today, albeit empty and out of use.

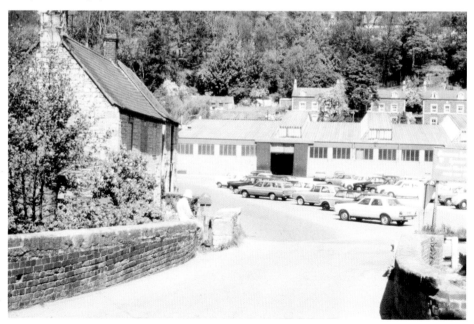

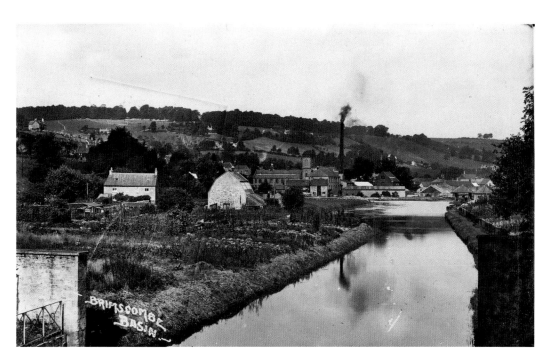

Leaving Brimscombe Port

Many views of the port look east; here, looking west, the coal island seems largely out of use and the basin empty. The retaining wall enclosing the port area on its southern side meets the canal at bottom left, and similarly in shadow on the northern side. Door openings in each wall created a sense of leaving the port area, a detail that caught the eye of Temple Thurston around 1911, not least for the profusion of 'cow-parsnip' growing on the bank. The southern side wall was restored in 2007/08.

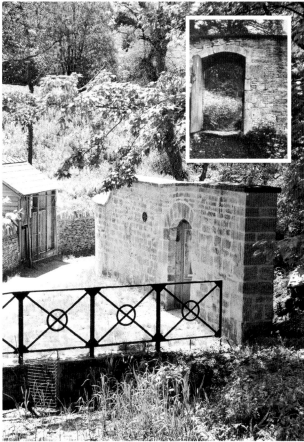

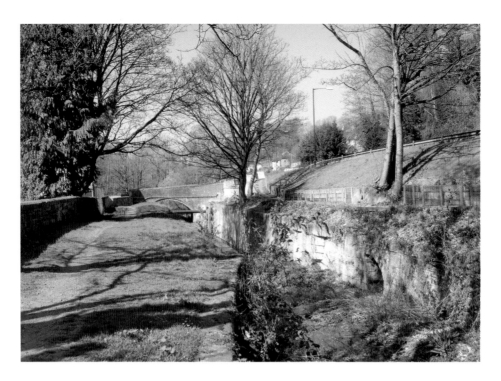

Bourne Mill & Lock

A hybrid lock at 90 feet long and 16 feet 1 inches wide, here in March 2012 tidied up in its 'rescued' if not yet restored state. Accessed over the canal bridge, the buildings at Bourne Mill were also restored in recent years, and are excellent examples of the great phase of mill rebuilding in 1825–50, with the woollen cloth industry at its height. It is a classic spot to appreciate the close proximity of road, canal and railway, competing for space along the valley; the railway appears to cut right through the group of mill buildings.

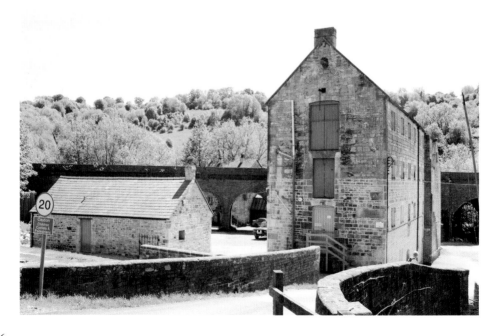

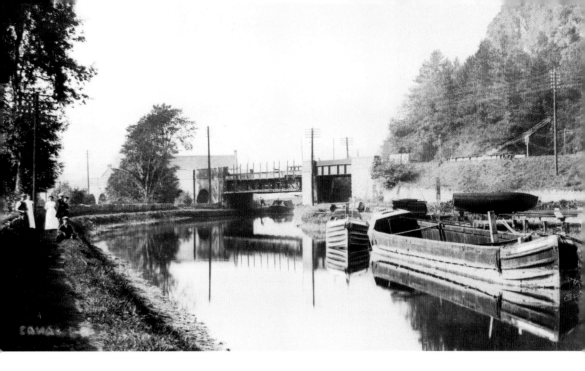

The Boatyard at Bourne

Boats are moored up at the entrance to the Bourne boatyard, another Thames & Severn focal point. Scant remains survived until recent years, factory buildings steadily covering the site, as seen here in May 1980. 'The Dockyard' name, however, seems to still be in use today! Originally the canal company's own yard, set up soon after the canal was opened, it was the scene of much boatbuilding and repairing activity in fairly simple conditions. Boats were constructed in a dry dock or on the canal bank, from where they were launched sideways into the cut.

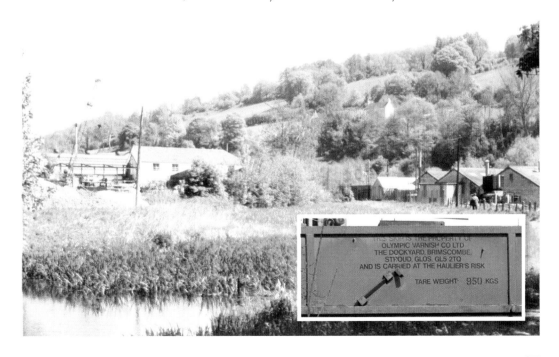

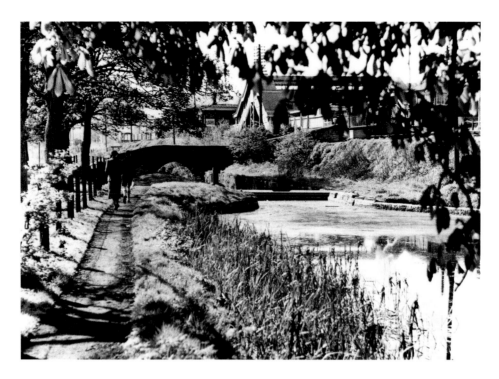

Beale's Lock & Pound

A delightful view in 1957 of the canal and railway, side by side, at Brimscombe station, with Beale's Lock and bridge in the foreground, looking west. The station was still functioning in typical ex-GWR fashion, with the canal full of water above the lock (held back by a concrete dam) to service the needs of the banker engines based at the station for Sapperton Bank duties. Although the canal is still in water today (seen again in May 1980), all evidence of the station has vanished completely.

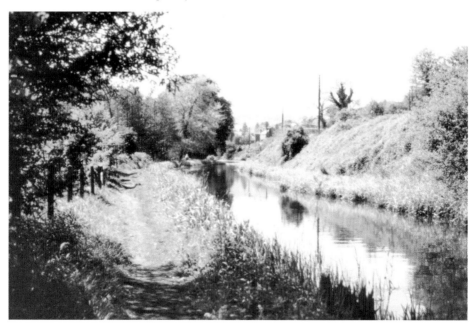

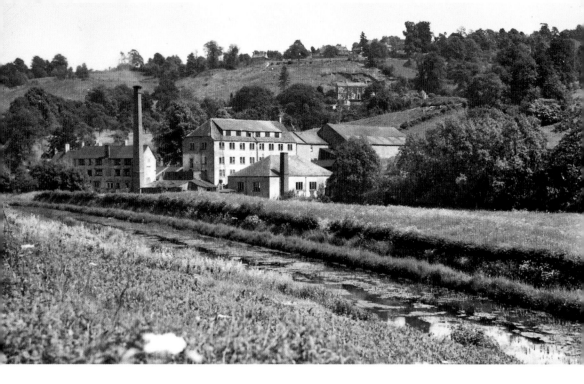

St Mary's Mill & Lock

Humphrey Household's fine record photograph from June 1947 of the pound in water between Beale's and St Mary's Locks. St Mary's Mill is a fine group of historic buildings, the mill house hidden behind. Until 1986, walking sticks were still being made here. Access is achieved via a tight descent from the main road across the only surviving manned railway crossing in the valleys, and certainly the most picturesque. The tiny crossing keeper's cabin, now a listed building, stands almost on top of the lock by the bridge.

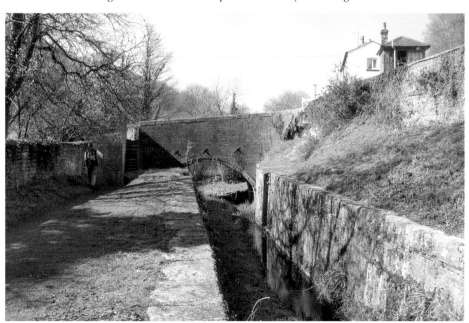

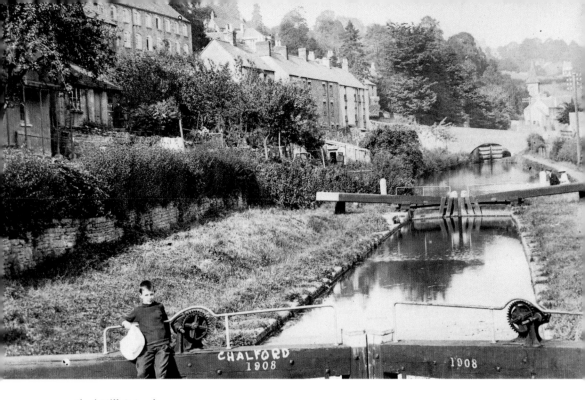

Iles' Mill & Lock

The locks now come closer together, as the canal climbs the valley. Just before the lock is Clayfield's Mill, now converted into housing and squeezed by road widening in the mid-1960s. A small stream, which emerges on the valley side, powered a waterwheel in the mill before entering the canal. From the bridge, the view across the lock is towards Ballinger's. The slatting on the lock gates is a Thames & Severn characteristic, the date 1908 on the lower gates is evidence of repair and refitting. This view dates from not long afterwards.

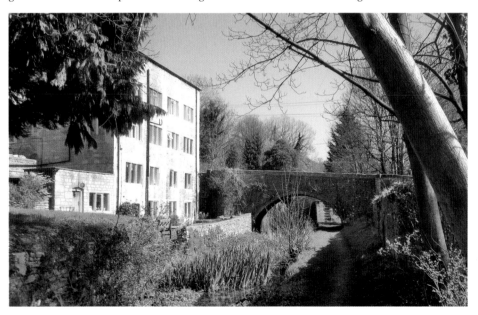

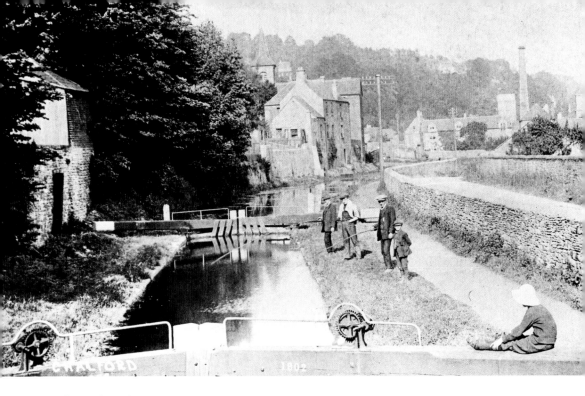

Ballinger's Lock

Another lock with evidence of repair and refitting, this time dated 1902. Beyond, buildings stand close to the canal side, one of the features most affected by road widening along the valley. The approach to Chalford wharf in the distance did benefit from a 'Stroud Valley Facelift' project in the mid-1960s; it is a pity that the infilled lock chamber is now covered by a small row of three garages, with the canal culverted beneath. Ballinger is another local family name associated with ownership of mills.

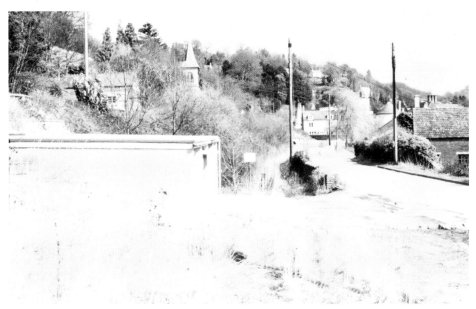

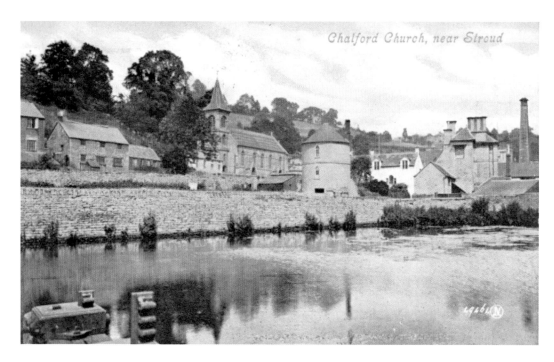

Chalford Wharf

Chalford wharf was a busy place with many mills in fairly close proximity; these views look across the mill pound of the adjoining Belvedere Mill. The location seems to have a timeless quality of its own, with the round house just below the road with Christ Church behind and the impressive part-fifteenth-century Chalford Place on the right, formerly the Company's Arms inn. The canal widened here to form a 'winding hole', or turning place, for barges.

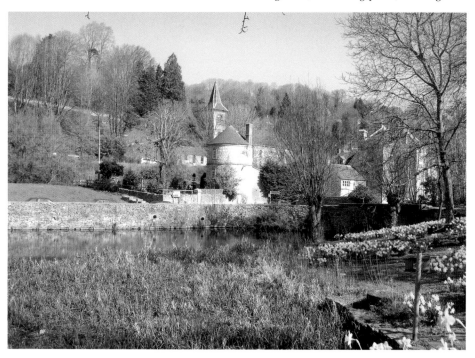

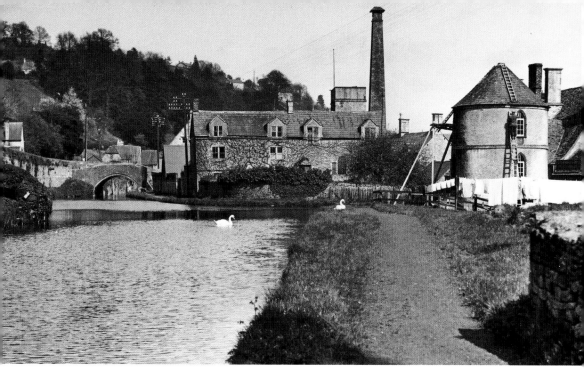

Chalford Wharf & Round House

Today the wharf represents a small but valuable amenity area. Its centrepiece is undoubtedly the round house, the first of five on the Thames & Severn, seen here on 29 April 1937. Beyond, the nearest house to the canal belonged to James Smart, bargemaster and coal merchant, whose firm had its own fleet of barges trading on the canals. The wedding group on 6 March 1926 is the Dowdeswell family. Great grandfather George (1829–1909) had worked as a labourer, lock-keeper, toll-keeper and lengthman for the canal company, finally settling in the round house.

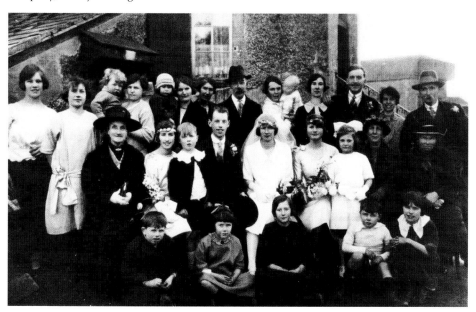

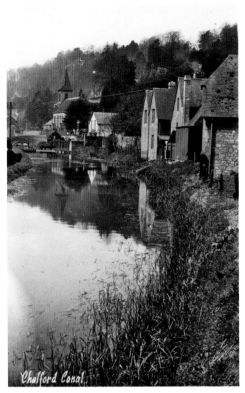

Chalford Canal

Chalford Chapel Lock

Above the bridge, the lock and this length
of canal and adjoining buildings, including
Couldrey's coal wharf, were cleared and
infilled in 1964 for road widening and
improvements, consuming around half of the
canal bed. Today, only the towpath remains as
a tree-lined walk. Behind the long stone wall
was the substantial group of buildings known
as Bliss' Mill, once five separate mill concerns
employing at their peak in excess of 1,000
people in the manufacture of walking sticks
and other products. The site now forms the
Chalford trading estate.

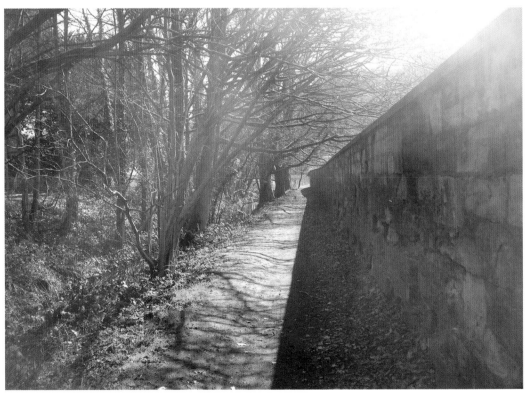

Bell Bridge

At the bottom of Cowcombe Hill, where the main road to Cirencester crosses the canal line, stood Bell Bridge, substantially built in stone in 1814 to carry the new turnpike road over the canal. It is photographed here in 1955. Although it looks today as if it too fell victim to the 1960s road improvements, the bridge does survive but it is hidden; the River Frome is culverted deep under the canal here. Hallidays mill building, part-brick part-stone, anchors the scene in the spring of 2012.

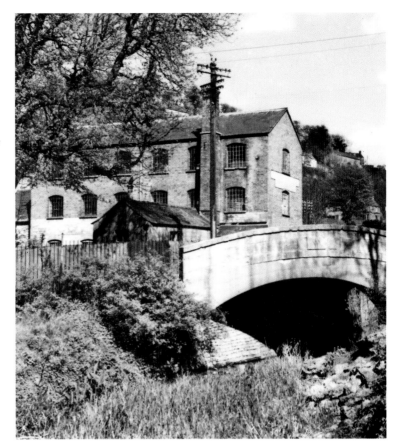

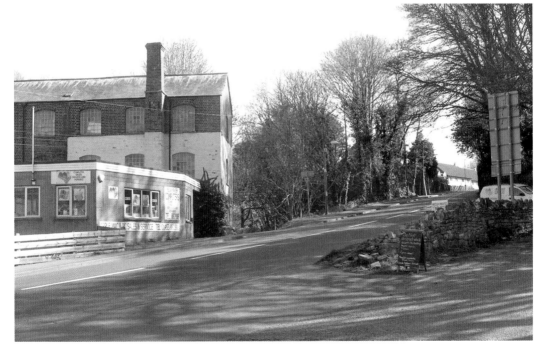

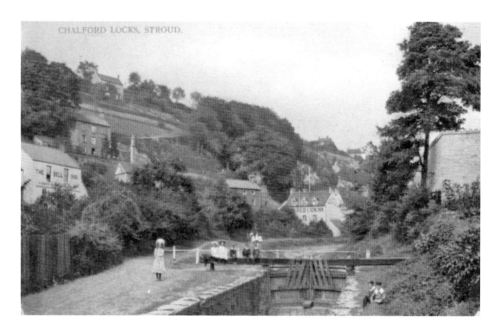

Bell Lock

Crossing from right to left, the towpath now seems to enter another world, with decreasing road noise, offering a tranquil 3-mile walk all the way to the summit at Daneway. This was among the most photographed locks along the canal in Edwardian times. Some of Bell Lock chamber survives. Its gates were replaced in 1904, the date marked on the beam. Of the two inns, the Bell Inn and the Red Lion further on, only the latter survives. The canal and towpath are captured on a fine April day in 2012.

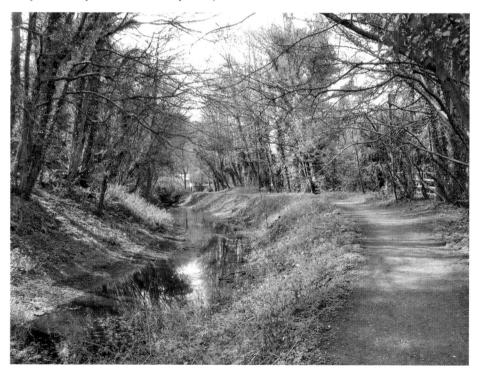

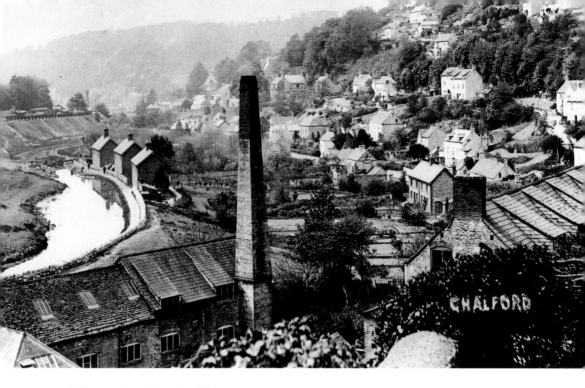

Red Lion Lock & Clowes' Bridge

As the original cutting of the canal line was advanced from west to east, it reached Red Lion Lock by late 1784, around eighteen months after work commenced. This significance is supported by construction of a fine example of a stone bridge across the tail of the lock, with its keystone inscribed, 'CLOWS ENGINr 1785'. Josiah Clowes was the canal company's 'surveyor, engineer and head carpenter' from 1783, and effectively its resident engineer. The milestone (*Walbridge 4½*) still stands alongside the lock, its plate with the characteristic single 'L' now preserved elsewhere.

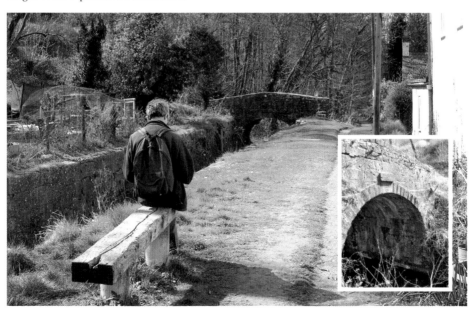

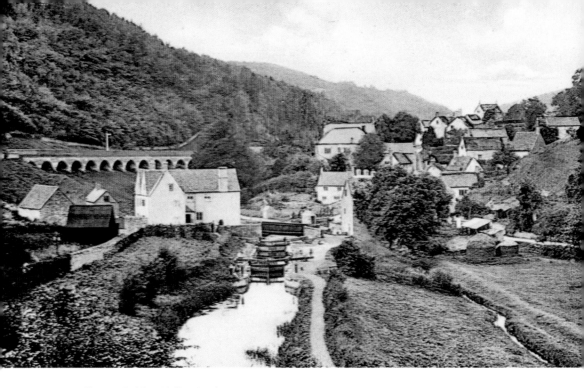

Valley or Golden Valley Lock

Around the bend is Golden Valley Lock, which together with the previous two locks has raised the canal through 26 feet in just half a mile. In this F. Major of Bisley postcard view from around 1910, lock, bridge and inn stand in the centre of another little valley-side community, with cottages and houses close together. Right by the lock and sharing its name stands the former Valley Inn. This late seventeenth-century Cotswold stone house was originally a mill house and its first name as a pub was the Clothiers Arms.

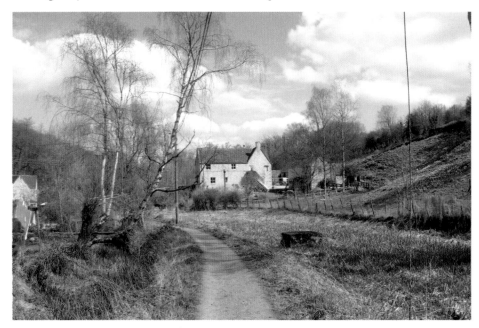

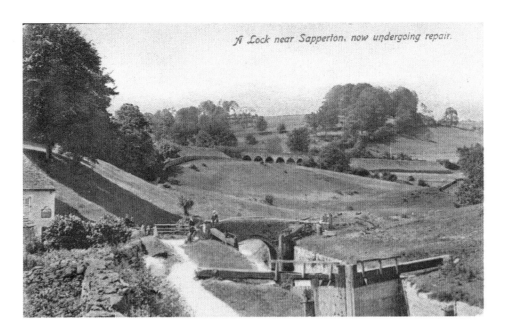

A Lock near Sapperton, now undergoing repair.

Puck Mill

This Woodbury Series postcard captures the charm and isolation of Puck Mill around 1903, showing the decayed state of the Upper Lock. The sign of the Oak Inn can just be seen on the left. The caption suggests an overprinting and reissuing of this earlier photograph once repair work had begun. Licensee Samuel Elliott and his wife Emily stand at the gate of the inn; this view was taken from the bridge across the Upper Lock. The advertising on the end gable wall and over the door leaves little room for doubt.

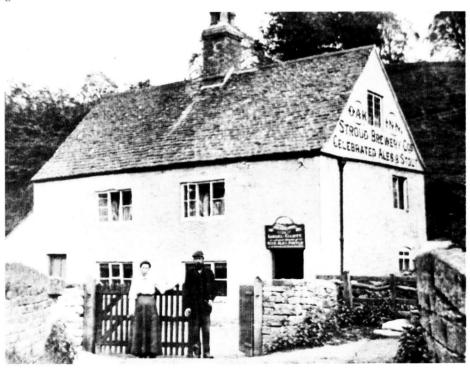

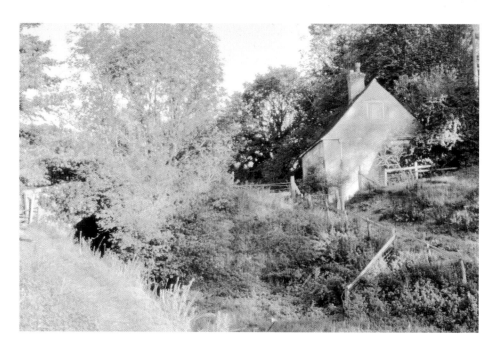

Puck Mill

The same building and view, looking up from below the bridge in October 1976 and again in April 2007. The old inn closed in February 1919, the Elliotts still in charge. Used for storage, it has since become a private house, suitably enlarged to benefit from its fine location. Puck Mill must have been an interesting little community gathered in the valley floor, with the canal as the main focus. Construction obviously split up the limited farming land in the valley, hence the need for an 'accommodation' bridge to link up the several portions.

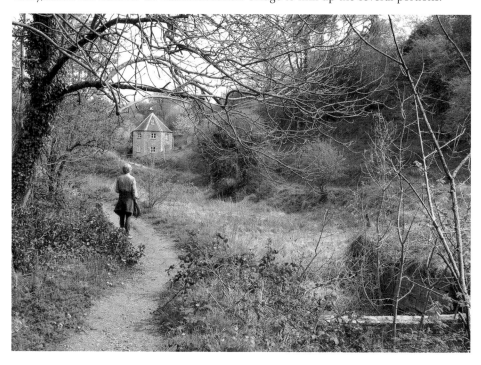

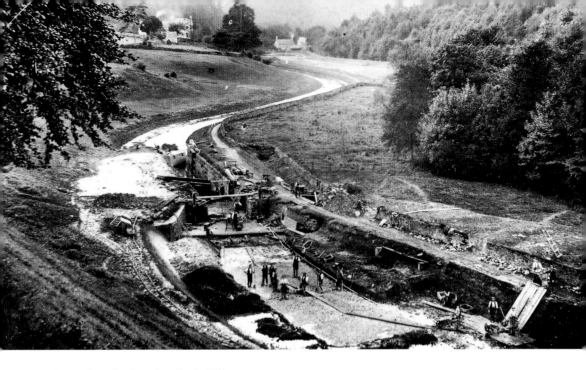

Restoring the Canal at Puck Mill

An intensive programme of reconstruction at Puck Mill Lower Lock and the pound above took place in 1907. Thankfully well recorded, one view looks down over the whole scene, with Baker's Mill in the background, while the other looks back up to the bridge and inn. The processes of lock repair and relining by puddling clay in the pound are clear to see and, with only minor changes of detail, replicate the way in which the canal must have been built and repaired throughout its life. A three-month closure from mid-August was required.

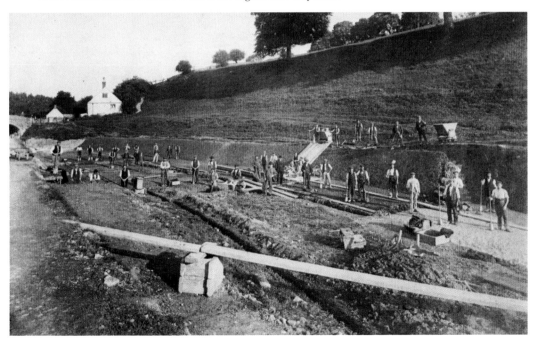

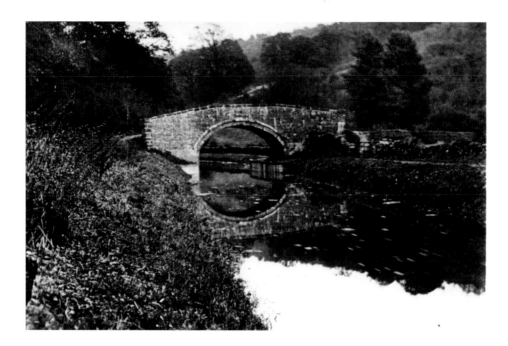

Whitehall Bridge

Isolated in the valley floor, Whitehall Bridge remains an impressive structure with much evidence of repair and rebuilding. Another accommodation bridge, it serves the several tracks and footpaths that cross at this point. On the lower side, a fine (if decaying) datestone reads, 'W. D. 1784', presumably named after the contractor-mason William Dennis, who was also responsible for some of the locks just above. Whitehall Bridge was the demarcation point for official abandonment of the canal to the east in 1927; the length to here from Wallbridge wasn't officially abandoned until 1933.

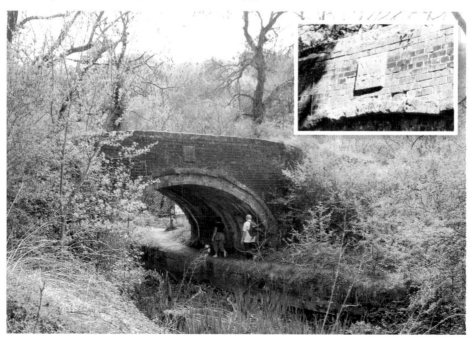

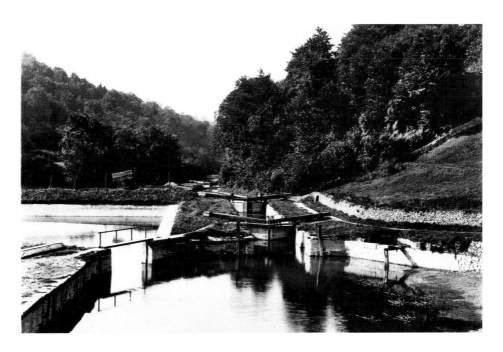

Climbing to Daneway

Between Puck Mill and Daneway, a distance of almost a mile, there are no more houses in the valley but there is still much of interest. The towpath is an enjoyable and popular walk up a flight of seven locks, all within the half-mile up to the summit level at Daneway, seen here around 1910. At last, the valley opens out to allow enough space for the wharf and basin, accessed just above Daneway Basin Lock. All the way up, the wood and tumbles down the hillsides on either bank, much of it now a nature reserve.

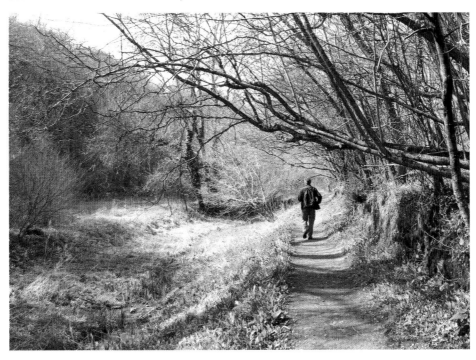

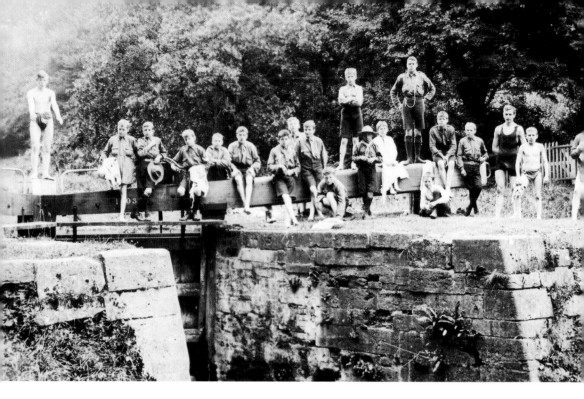

Climbing to Daneway

Diving skills on show here at one of the Daneway flight of locks; this is believed to be a scout group from Woodchester. Swimming in locks along the canal was a popular pastime whenever there was enough water! In its working days this section of canal often presented difficulties. The pounds (reservoirs, really) were built too short to contain the amount of water required to fill each lock. The view from Daneway Banks in April 2007 takes in the almost-hidden basin site, the inn and the road straggling up towards Sapperton village.

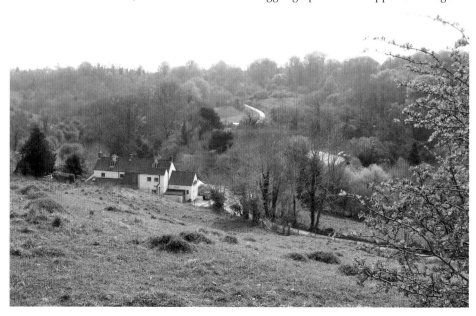

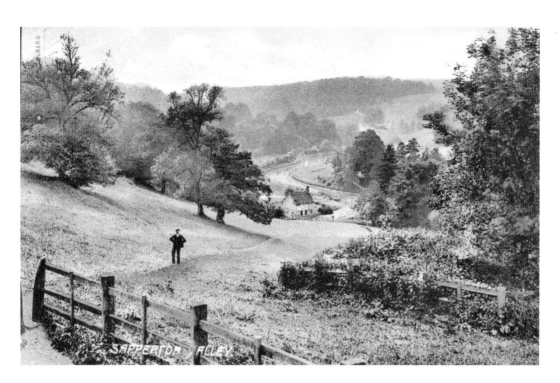

Reaching the Summit at Daneway

Cirencester photographer W. Dennis Moss captured this scene on the path down from Sapperton village, looking to the canal watchman's cottage by the tunnel entrance, now alas demolished. Beyond is the Daneway Inn, previously called the Bricklayers Arms, its long-standing tradition of whitewash more readily apparent from the same spot on 2 April 2012.

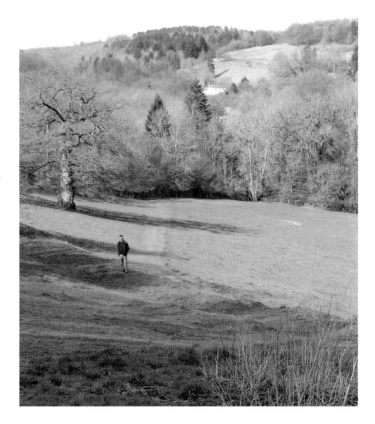

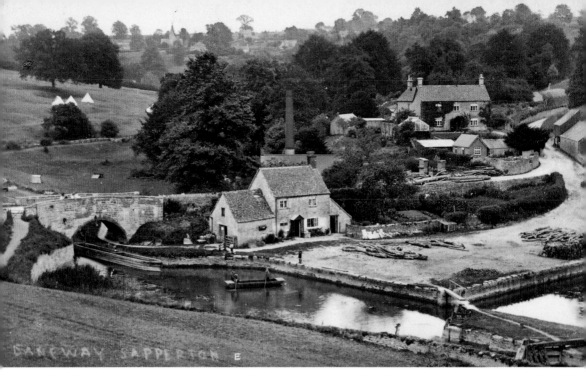

DANEWAY SAPPERTON E

Daneway Wharf & Basin

Very early on, this little canal-side community at the start of the summit level became a hive of activity, with the establishment of an inn, wharf, warehouse and coal yard, plus the construction of the road now running up the valley side to Sapperton village on the skyline. In the centre of this view is the wharf cottage, with the open expanse of wharf in front and the basin to the right. Behind, the tall brick sawmill chimney is partially hidden by trees. By August 1979, the wharf cottage has been restored and the inn lies behind.

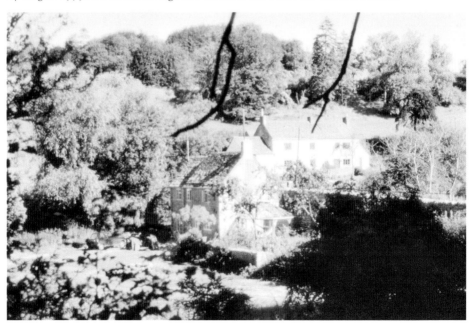

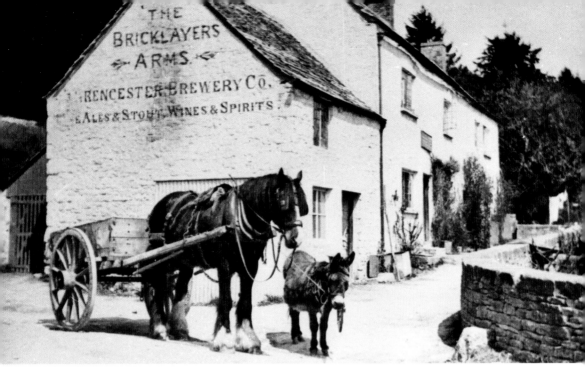

Daneway Inn & Lock

The inn was built by canal contractor John Nock in 1784 as a base and accommodation for his men working on the construction of nearby Sapperton tunnel. Sold out of Canal Company ownership in 1807 to become the Bricklayer's Arms inn, it has been a public house ever since and was renamed the Daneway Inn in 1947. Thirty years before, on 8 May 1917, horse and donkey wait patiently outside for their master. Daneway Top Lock has been infilled to form the car park, seen here in October sunshine in 1976.

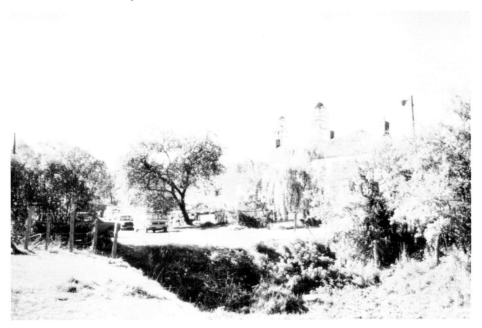

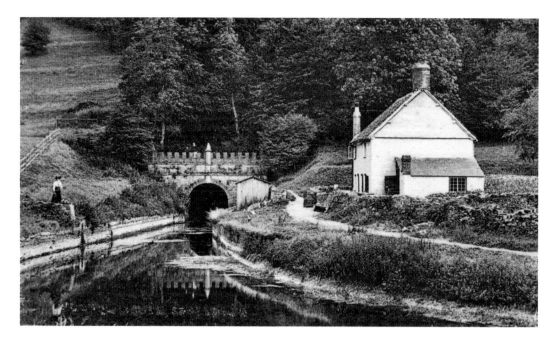

Daneway Portal of the Sapperton Tunnel

The Daneway entrance to Sapperton tunnel is probably the best known of the postcard views along the Thames & Severn Canal. These are the work of local photographers F. Major of Bisley (above) and F. Colville of Chalford (below). The pair of stone cottages at the entrance to the tunnel were lived in until the 1970s, despite being some way from the nearest road. Beyond, the gloom and mystery of the tunnel beckons, approached on a bend as the line of the tunnel through the hills was surveyed first.

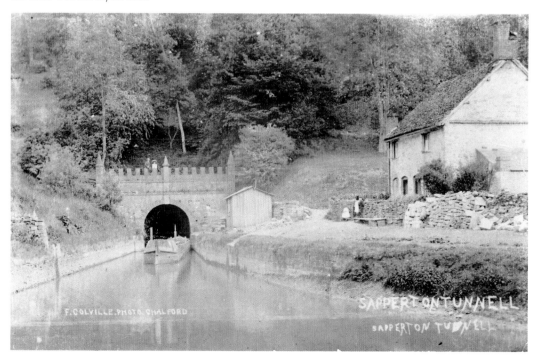

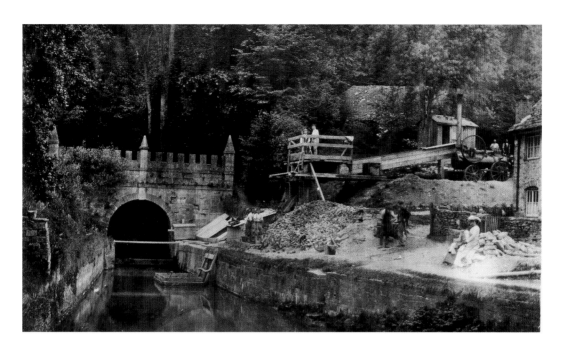

Daneway Portal of the Sapperton Tunnel

Contractors are at work around 1903 in the early years of Gloucestershire County Council ownership of the canal. Clay is being crushed for use in the canal bed with the tunnel blocked off by wooden stop-planks. Humphrey Household captured a superb view of the tunnel setting in May 1947. A significant achievement in recent years has been the restoration of the tunnel portal or façade, which was completed in September 1996, returning to its former impressive state the battlemented entrance full of gloom and foreboding. It presents a sombre image to the canal traveller.

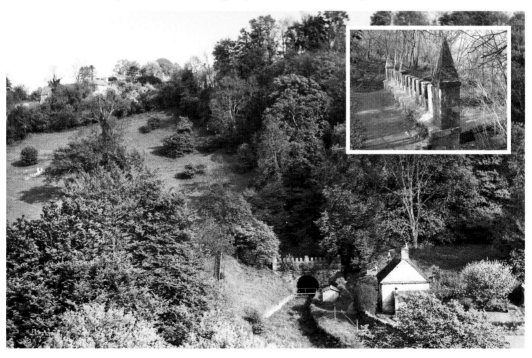

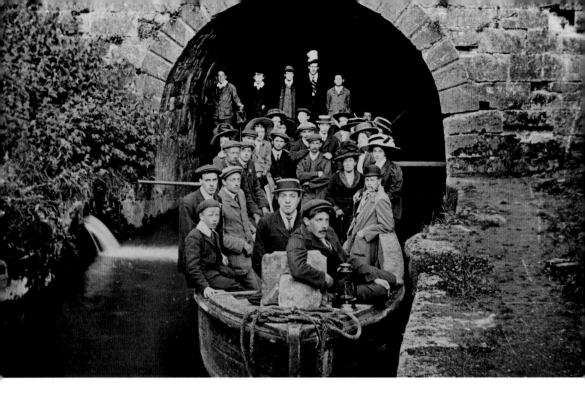

Sapperton Tunnel

The sense of awe with which boatmen and later visitors, such as these from Brimscombe Polytechnic, entered the darkness of the tunnel can still be appreciated. Certainly the most impressive achievement in the canal's construction, it was also the most difficult and expensive. It took five years to construct, driving a 15-foot-diameter tunnel over 2 miles long, with twenty-five vertical shafts, at a depth below the surface of 200 feet in places. Until blockages occurred, it was apparently possible in places to see right through the tunnel, but is now securely sealed for safety reasons.

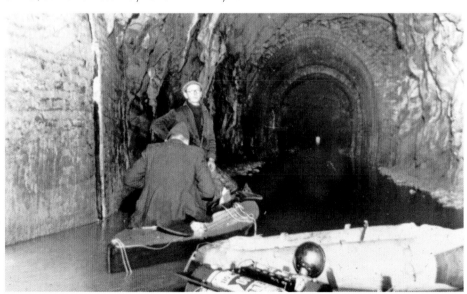

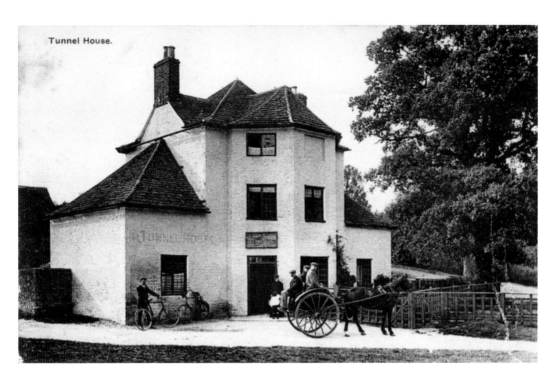

Tunnel House.

Tunnel House Inn at Coates

Immediately above the Coates portal, and like the Daneway Inn that is happily still in use as a pub, the Tunnel House Inn also belongs to the construction period of the canal, being built as accommodation for workers. It was then called the New Inn and had a range of stabling behind, all now cleared away. Perhaps the greatest tragedy was a severe fire in January 1952, which gutted the building. It was reconstructed over several years as it is now, without its original third floor that had served as lodging accommodation.

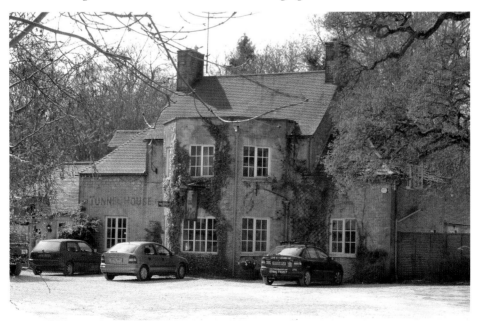

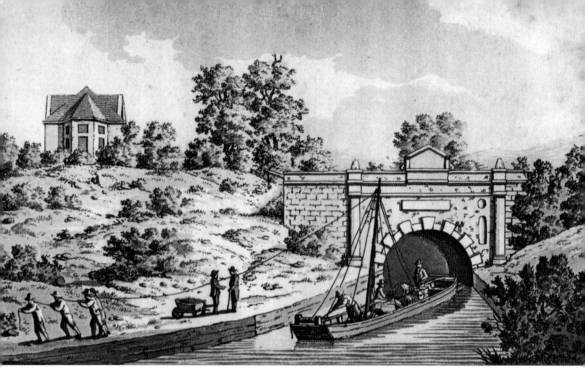

Coates Portal of the Sapperton Tunnel

The Coates portal remains an impressive structure as probably it was always intended to be something of a showpiece for the Thames & Severn. With Tunnel House up on the bank, this 1790 sketch by Samuel Ireland makes just that point. The detailing is a sort of checklist of classical-style features, a pediment with flanking columns and finials plus niches and circular roundels, all set above a tunnel mouth well down into the cut. The depressing scene in January 1972 shows the need for restoration of the whole façade.

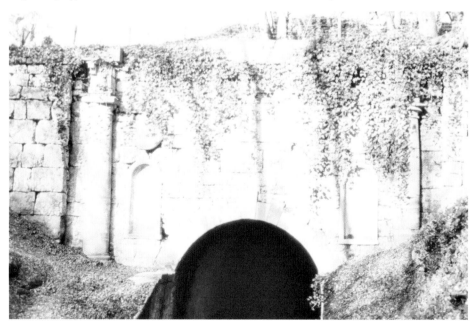

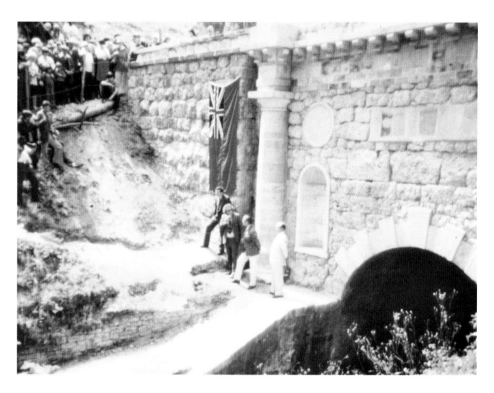

Restoring Coates Portal of the Sapperton Tunnel

Cotswold Canals Trust raised funds for the portal's restoration, recovering much of the masonry from the canal bed for repair and reuse. A relatively small amount of new stone was used, now long blended in with the original. The formal unveiling by Earl Bathurst in July 1977 remains one of the highlights of restoration so far. The whole section continues to do its job, although the façade is once again showing signs of decay.

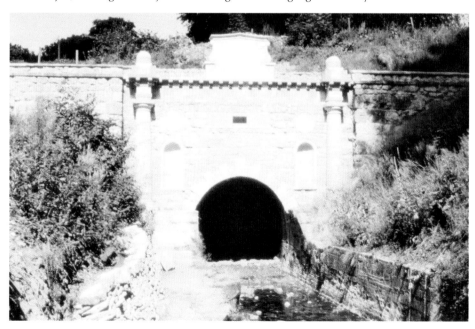

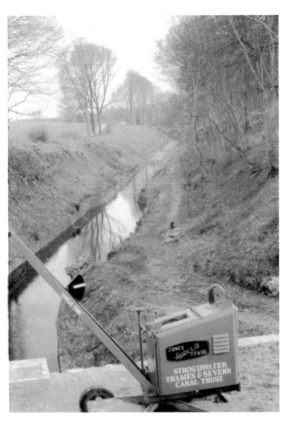

The King's Reach

The cutting stretches away from the tunnel in a straight line, known as the King's Reach following a visit by King George III in July 1788 when he 'expressed the most decided astonishment and commendation' at the work in progress. At the tunnel entrance is a barge lay-by for vessels awaiting their turn to navigate through. An umbrella of beech trees sheltered the cutting for many years but clearance of dead trees and renewal during 1976 dramatically opened it up, as seen here in both directions on 11 March 1978.

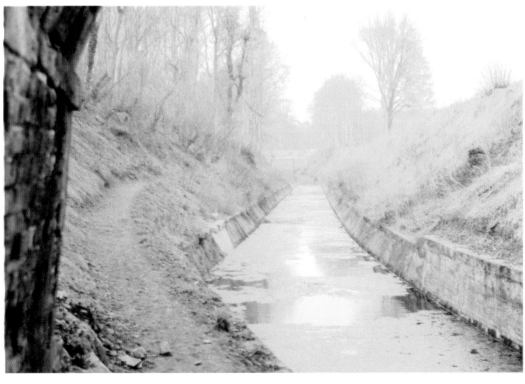

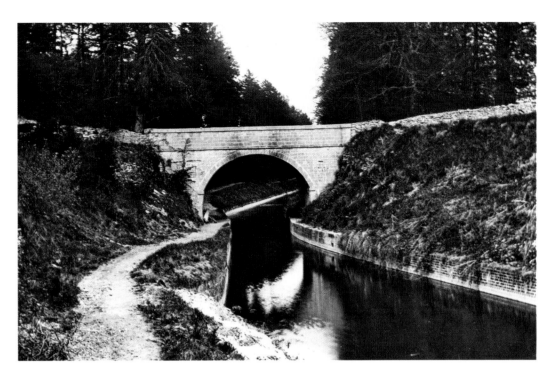

Tarlton Road Bridge

Tarlton Road Bridge is another fine structure, rebuilt in stone in 1823 and an impressive counterpoint at the end of King's Reach. It is kept in good condition as a highway bridge and seems to sit comfortably in its landscape. In the reach beyond, the concrete relining of the canal is visible, dating from Gloucestershire County Council's period of restoration from 1900 onwards, part of the battle against water leakage through fissures in the rock. The concrete lining here was a complete success, but too costly to extend further.

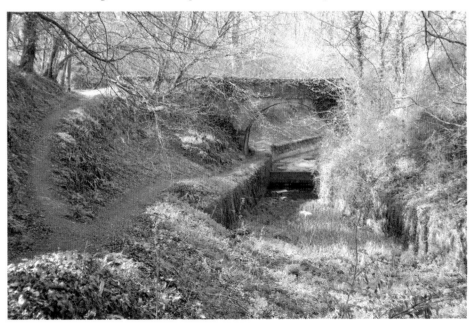

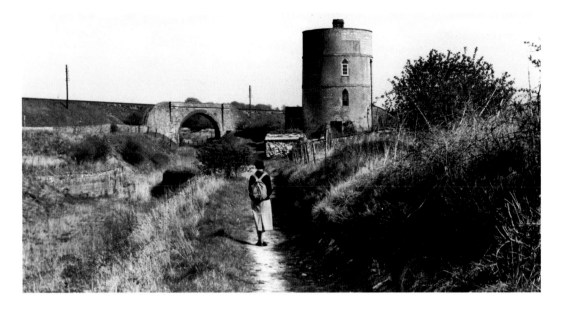

Towards Coates Round House

The canal now reverts to a west/east alignment along the summit level towards Coates round house, with the railway 'skew' bridge beyond. Here are echoes of the original surveyor Robert Whitworth's prediction of 'bad, rocky ground', drawing water away through the fissures in the rock. In response, an important feature of water-management arrangements were the single self-acting gates, provided from the outset at five points along the summit level, as here, to protect this all-important reservoir and limit losses when leaks developed. These two views date from 1938 and April 2010.

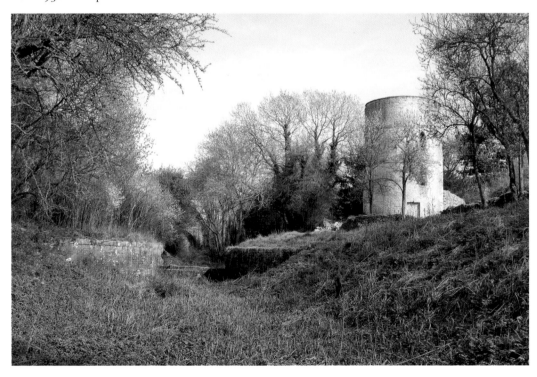

Coates Round House

A very interesting comparison with the example at Chalford, the Coates round house has the same dimensions and internal layout but a different roof construction. Instead of the upright conical shape, the roof here (and on two other round houses) was inverted, the whole arrangement concealed behind the circular wall of the building. In such an isolated spot as Coates, this was the most successful way of gathering a water supply, piped off the roof into water storage at ground level. In August 1949 the building was still occupied and conversion of the ground floor from stable to living accommodation can be seen, although the first-floor entrance remains in use. It is derelict now, as seen here in April 2010.

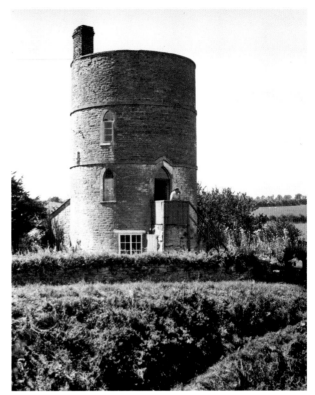

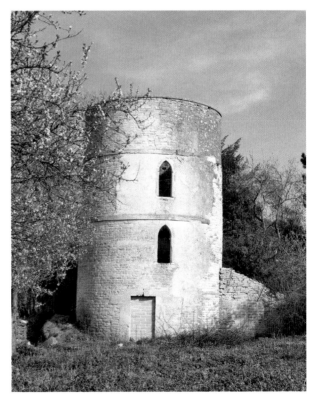

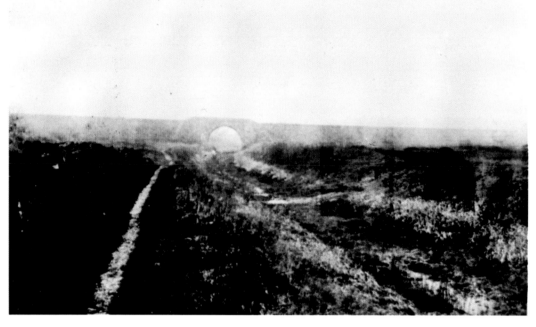

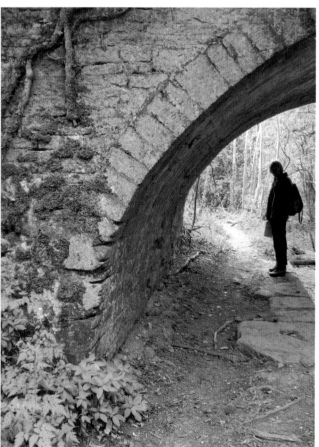

Along the Summit to Thames Head

A bleak view between Trewsbury and Coates, showing the canal in poor state and the railway crossing in the background. This is another from de Salis's survey of the Thames & Severn in 1896, while studying the general state of the canal system. Seeking greater efficiency, he must have pondered the scale of the challenge on these higher sections of the Thames & Severn. Just beyond, at Coatesfield Bridge, is clear evidence of the straining towing lines making their mark on the bridge, which bends sharply yet again, following the contour of the canal line.

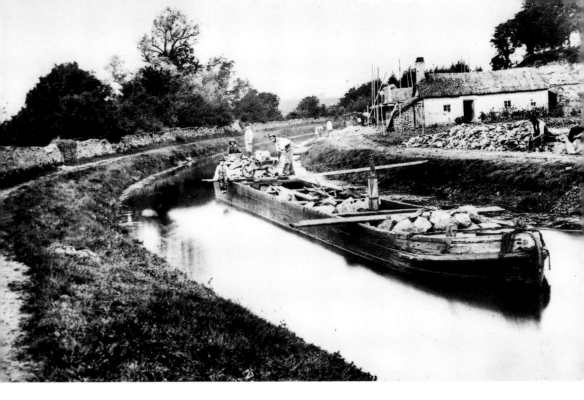

Thames Head Wharf

A boatload of Cotswold stone is being loaded alongside the quarry at Coatesfield in this rare view of localised canal-side trading around 1878–85. Nearby, alongside the main Cirencester to Bath road, is the small community and roadside wharf at Thames Head, intended to attract traffic from Tetbury and beyond. There was a wharf house, small warehouse and some stables, with a resident company agent here until around 1835 when the amount of trade could no longer justify his retention. Various buildings survive, as does Thames Head Bridge, which was saved when the road was realigned in 1962.

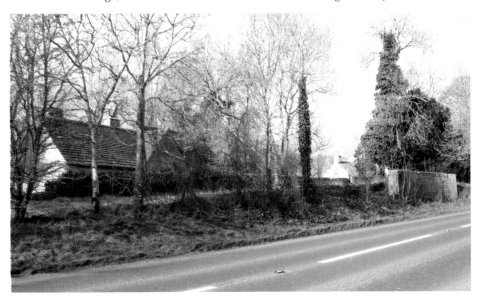

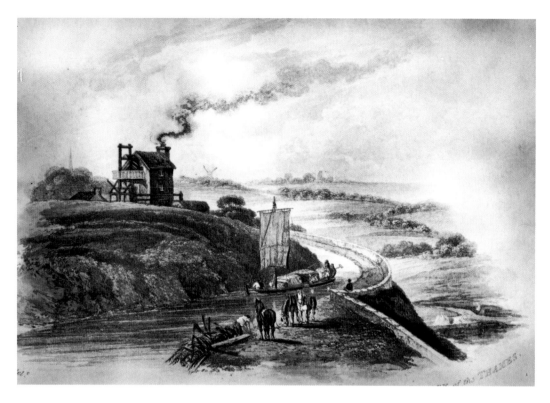

Thames Head Pump

The need to pump water into the summit level was obvious from the start. This Boulton & Watt single acting beam engine, seen from the road in 1828, remained in use from 1792 until 1854. Below is Henry Taunt's view of the Cornish engine that replaced it in 1854, making a dramatic improvement to the pumping operation. It was in service for over fifty years, until navigation in the summit level was all but over. It was scrapped in 1941 as part of the war effort.

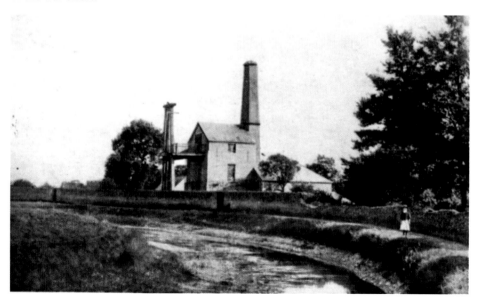

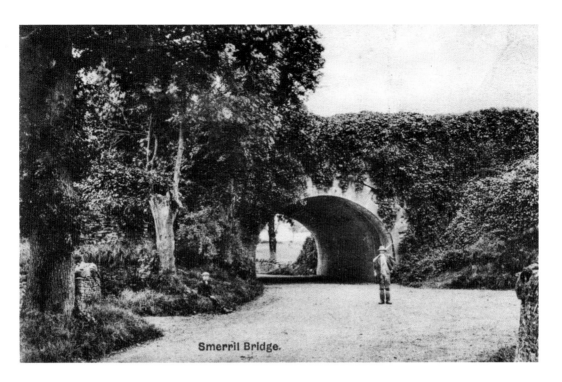

Smerrll Bridge.

Smerrill Aqueduct

The single-arched masonry structure of Smerrill Aqueduct over the Cirencester to Malmesbury road can be seen in this postcard view from around 1914, which looks towards Kemble. Once the canal had closed in 1927, the removal of this obstruction to traffic increased in priority and it was soon cleared away. Some thirty years later, further road improvements were made at Smerrill by cutting back the embankment and widening the road to create the present alignment, this view also looking towards Kemble.

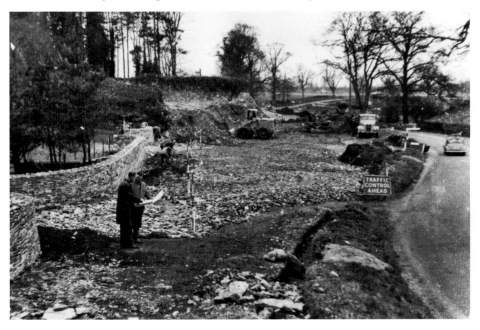

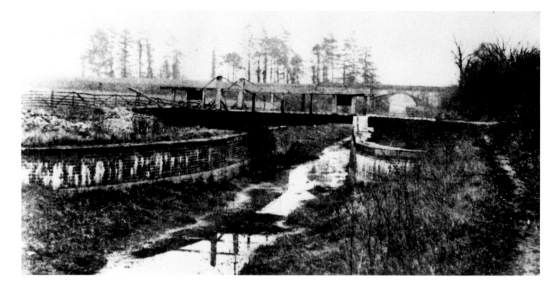

Along Towards Furzenleaze

The canal line is now less easy to trace, with much cleared away after closure including this swing bridge east of Smerrill, giving access between fields around 1896. In the background is the GWR branch to Cirencester. Just beyond, Halfway accommodation bridge survives, at approximately the mid-point between Wallbridge and Inglesham, and was splendidly rebuilt in 1997. At Bluehouse by Furzenleaze was a bridge and lengthman's cottage. There was considerable activity here in 1902–04 when contractors cut the clay for re-puddling the canal along this notoriously leaky summit level, as recorded by Henry Taunt of Oxford.

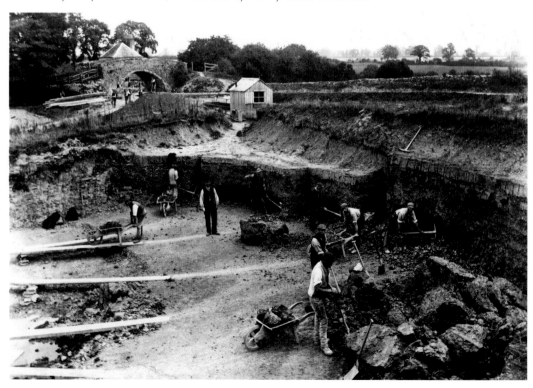

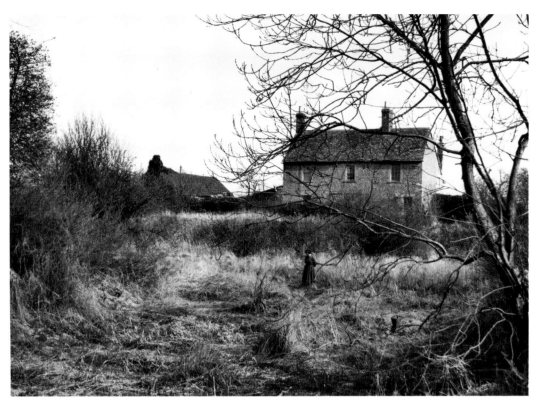

Siddington Junction

Another significant point on the Thames & Severn, the junction at Upper Siddington marked the eastern end of the summit level and the point at which the arm to Cirencester went off, to the left in this view of 1961 with Wharf House in the background and workshops and stables beyond. The Cirencester link allowed the town's trade to contribute to the canal's economy, and also extended the length of the summit level and its function as a reservoir, via access to water supplies and in particular the River Churn. Canal House survives today.

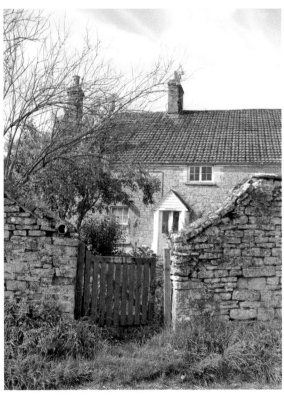

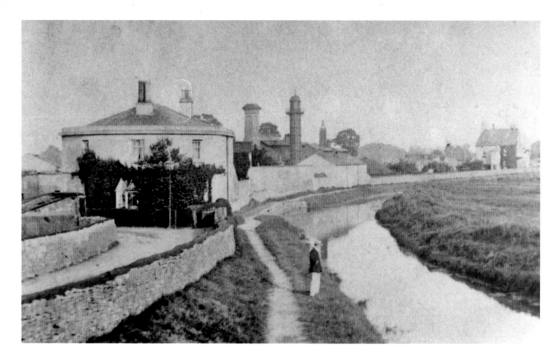

The Arm into Cirencester

Although only just over a mile in length, much of the canal line into Cirencester has been lost, as a result of the great changes around the town's southern edges. These two views date from 1907 and 1970, looking south from Chesterton Lane Bridge, with the town gasworks and its fine gas house of 1833 visible; the isolation hospital is further down the towpath. Other than the gas house, very little survives today, amid a sea of light industry, a highways depot and warehousing. Only with difficulty can the canal line be traced.

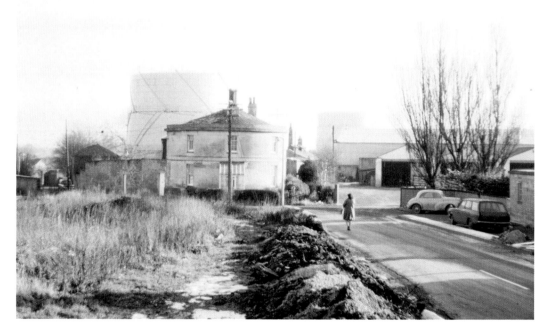

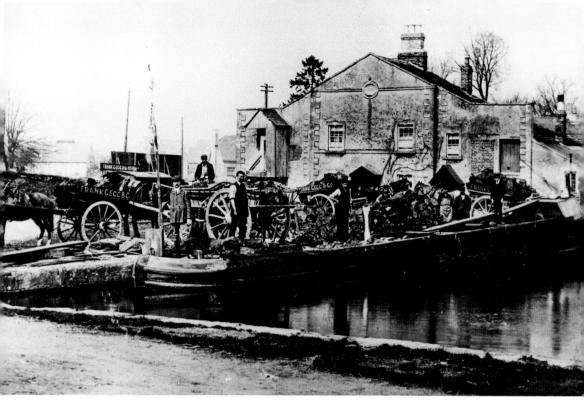

Cirencester Basin & Wharf

Nothing now survives of Cirencester wharf, a modern building covering the triangular site where Querns Road, Querns Lane and Querns Hill meet. As a terminal basin at the head of the arm, the wharf boasted quite a range of buildings including a fine warehouse, one of three to this design along the canal. A local 'event' following the reopening of the canal after closure was the arrival of *Staunch*, seen unloading 37 tons of Staffordshire coal on 19 March 1904. Local coal merchant Frank Gegg has utilised every available vehicle.

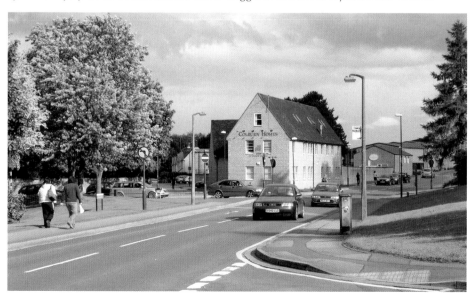

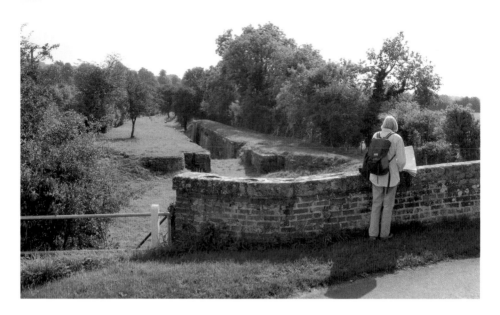

Siddington Locks

The brick bridge at the top of the locks is a good vantage point to contemplate the remaining 13½ miles descending to the Thames. A functioning highway bridge, which was repaired in 1988, it includes some interesting details, with iron clamps stamped 'TSC' holding the parapet coping stones in position. The group of four locks in quick succession take the canal 39 feet down from the summit level. These two views bear witness to a maturing long-term maintenance project, looking down the flight in September 2010 and looking up eleven years previously in September 1999.

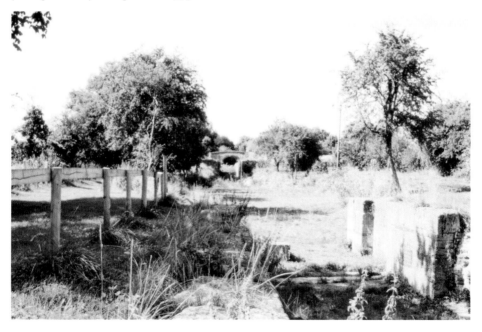

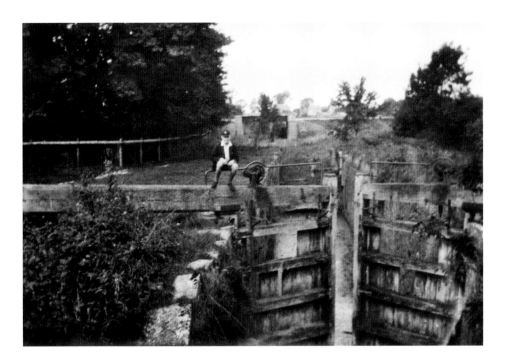

Siddington Locks and Beyond

Below where the former MSWJR line crossed, changes have been more significant. Siddington Bottom Lock, where the schoolboy here was photographed sitting on the lower gate balance beam, has long been infilled and a house now stands on this site. Behind the photographer, Greyhound Bridge has been levelled and from here, on a good length of maintained towpath, opens up all the way to Latton junction, some 5 miles away. This charming lower view sets the scene around 1915, looking back to Greyhound Bridge, which is still extant.

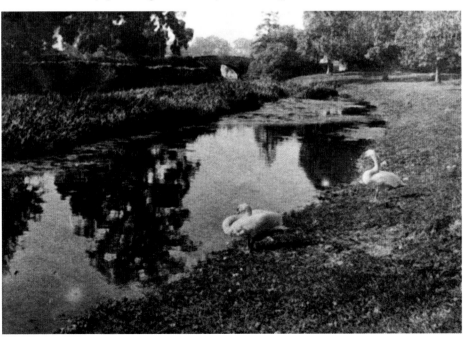

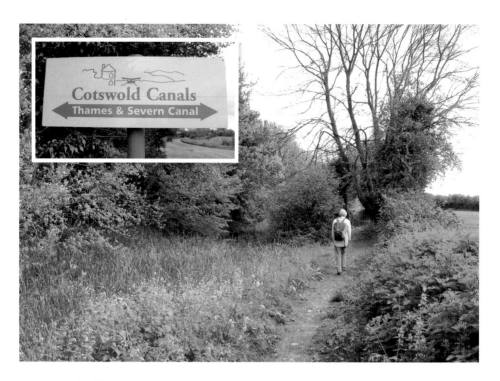

Cowground Bridge

Once beyond Siddington, the canal bed continues to hold water fairly well (from the gravel beds beneath) and there is a general encouragement of wildlife. If only for this reason, this is a delightful section to wander along. The isolated and attractive Cowground Bridge, another original humpback bridge in brick and stone, has enjoyed Trust-organised restoration, firstly of its collapsing arch and side walls, and more recently moving towards completing the parapet repairs. Here, the small but dedicated band is at work during 2012.

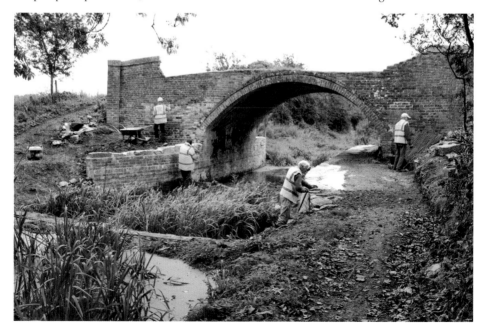

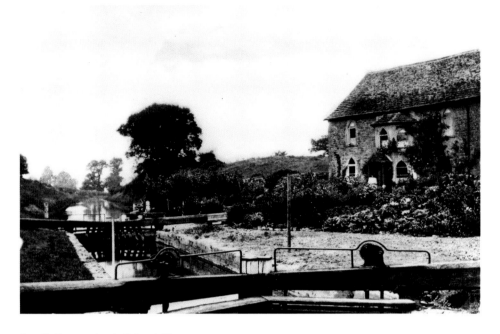

South Cerney Lock & Lock House

After a distance, a sharp turn takes the canal through the deep Claymeadow cutting to reach South Cerney wharf, and meets the Cirencester to South Cerney road. This was very much a local canal wharf at the roadside and some way out from the village, which was not unusual in the canal (and even the railway) period. South Cerney enjoyed a lock-keeper, who was responsible for the wharf and also acted as lengthman. The interesting bay window gives a good view over the lock, which today is cleverly and neatly preserved within the garden of the modernised property.

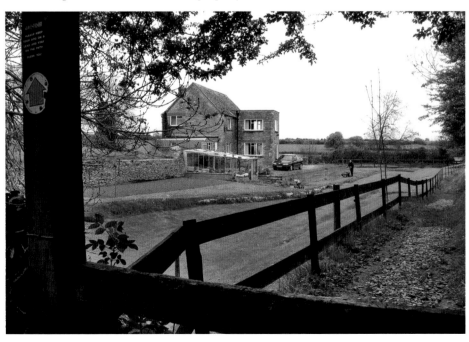

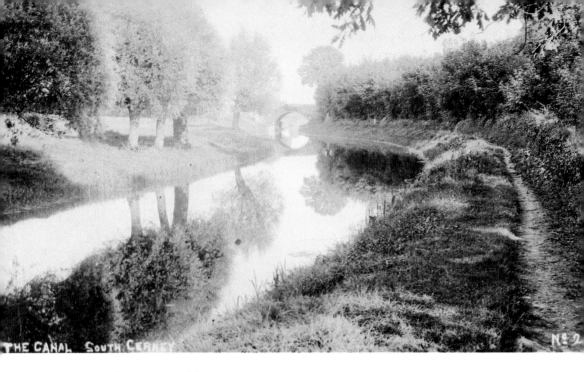

THE CANAL SOUTH CERNEY

No 2

Approaching Crane Bridge

Today, from Cerney wharf to Northmoor Lane is farmland, with the other two Cerney locks filled in. Presumably they remain reasonably intact and might once again be restored. Although there is relatively little by way of physical remains, the towpath nevertheless provides a leisurely walk towards Crane Bridge, which has since been levelled. These two views are some forty years apart, the first being the work of a local unnamed photographer and the second taken by Humphrey Household on 8 April 1947.

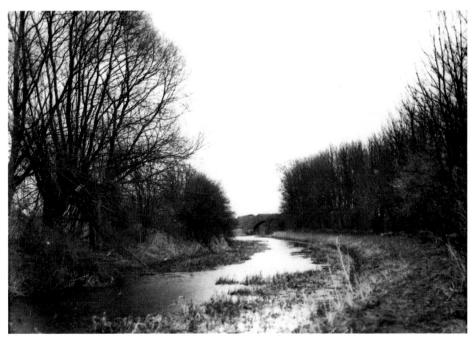

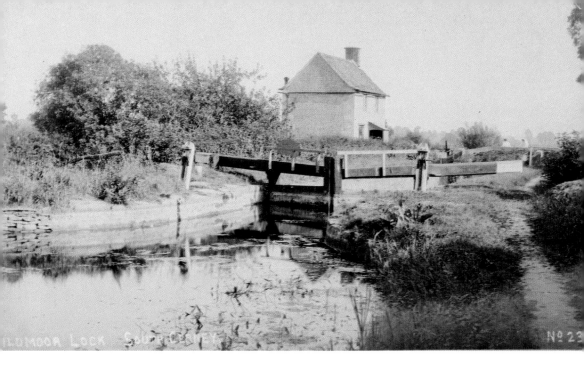

LDMOOR LOCK SOUTH CERNEY   Nº23

Wilmoreway Lock, Bridge & Lock Cottage

The modern spelling of this interesting place name is Wildmoorway but the version preferred in Thames & Severn Company records was the more phonetic Wilmoreway. Here the lower of two locks had a fall of 11 feet creating a combined fall of 18 feet 6 inches and a considerable water supply problem. A large stone-lined side pond was built here in 1831, the other precaution being a new lockside cottage for the lock-keeper moved here from Cerney Wick. At least a century apart, these views show the cottage, latterly in March 2011 after it was recently privately rebuilt.

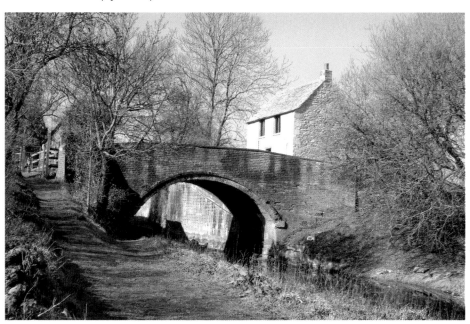

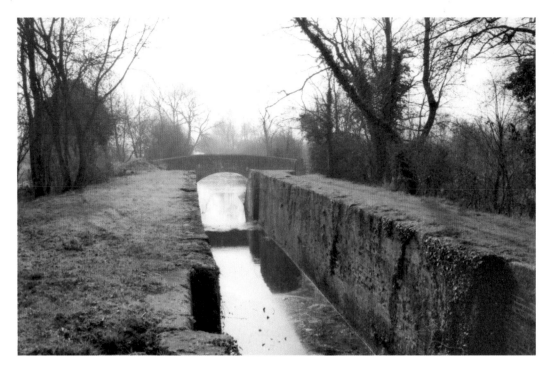

Wilmoreway Lock, Bridge & Lock Cottage

Wilmoreway Lower Lock and its accompanying brick bridge were the subject of a large-scale 'Dig Deep' working party blitz in 1995. The bridge looks almost new (complete with 1996 date stone), and the lock is one of the best examples on the Cotswold canals of careful reconstruction. Below, there is a short but attractive section of canal in water down to the Spine Road where the life and traffic of the Cotswold Water Park really begins to impact on the canal scene.

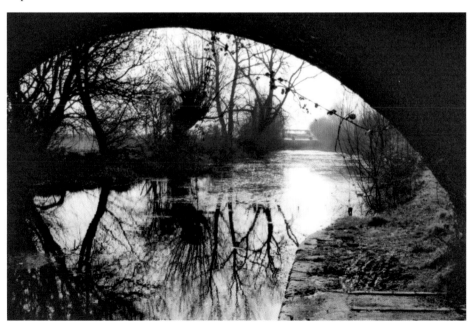

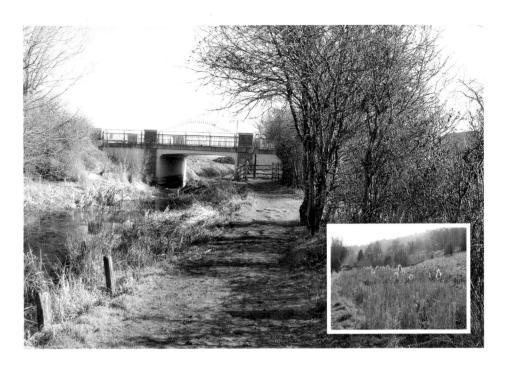

The Spine Road New Bridge

Another campaign success is the new Gateway Bridge where Spine Road crosses the canal, built in 2004 as a British Waterways/Cotswold Canals Partnership project. Approaching from Wilmoreway, one of the Thames & Severn milestones (unhappily now without its plate and broken in two) stands by the towpath. Could it not be restored? The bridge design in concrete and brick also adds something to the landscape; a sweeping flow of bulrushes graduated in thickness and made in stainless steel forms the side frames overlooking the canal. More such efforts where appropriate elsewhere, please!

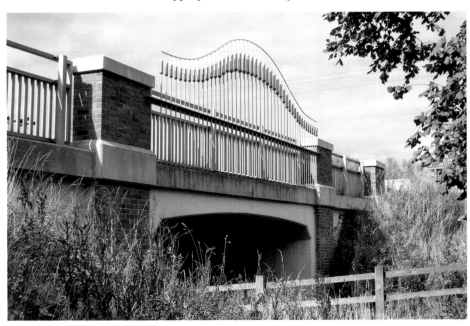

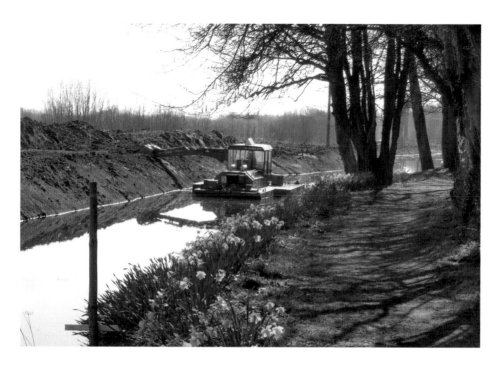

Dredging and Restoration

Considerable restoration along this Water Park section towards Cerney Wick is seen here in the spring sunshine of March 2011. The floating dredger has been very active. Clearing and re-watering the canal can help alleviate flooding, but relies upon access to funds and sponsorship for equipment as well as volunteers, the ability to resolve leaks and upgrade the towpath, plus an awareness throughout of environmental issues – particularly, in this case, satisfactory wildlife surveys. A spill weir, to release surplus water from this pound into the adjoining brook, has also been restored.

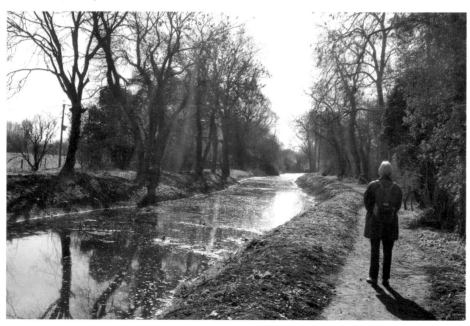

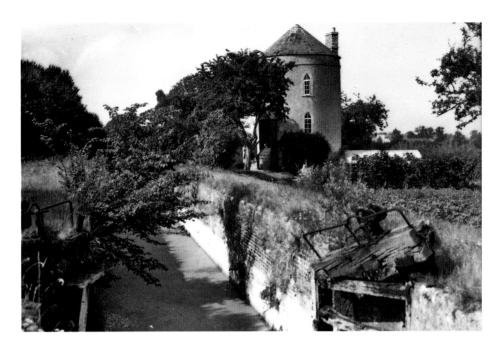

Cerney Wick Round House

This is the third of the canal's five round houses and one of its most attractive, seen here with the lock in dereliction on 18 August 1947 (Household again), and then in sunshine on 19 March 2011. Remarkably well preserved and looked after by its present owners, its original layout can still be appreciated: a ground-floor stable, a living room entered directly from external steps to the first floor, and upper-floor bedrooms. Similar familiar characteristics are the stone structure, faced with stucco, the narrow Gothic-style windows and the conical slate roof.

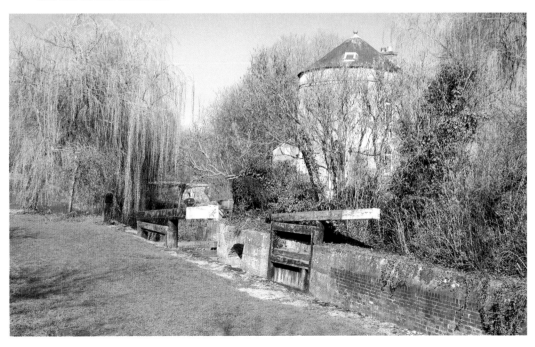

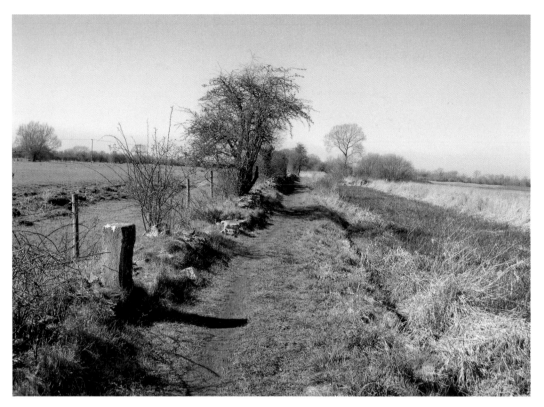

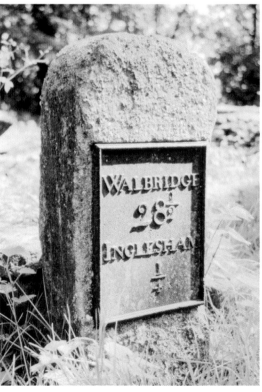

Milestones Along the Canal

The section to Latton through relatively featureless farmland also preserves examples of the canal's milestones. This marks 20 miles, measured from Wallbridge in Stroud. Both flat-topped and round-headed examples are found, and the final stone at Inglesham is complete with plate. Carriage of goods on the canal system was chargeable by tonnage and distance carried, a sender paying freight to the carrier and a toll to the canal company. Information on the length of any given journey was important and canal legislation required mileposts to be fixed on the banks so that tolls could be calculated.

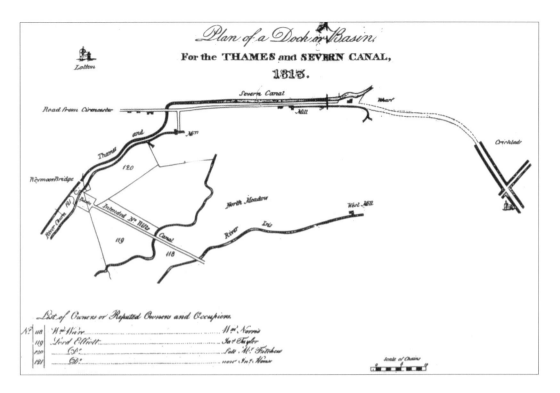

Plan of a Dock or Basin.
For the **THAMES** and **SEVERN CANAL,**
1813.

Latton Junction

As anticipated in this 1813 plan, Latton junction was a typical canal enterprise, linking two routes for mutual benefit. The 9-mile length of the North Wilts Canal linked the Thames & Severn Canal with the Wilts & Berks Canal at Swindon, providing an alternative and easier access to the Thames at Abingdon and avoiding the navigation problems of the upper reaches of the river to Lechlade. A painting of 1920 records the T-junction with the link into the basin under the bridge to the right and the 'main line' through Weymoor Bridge.

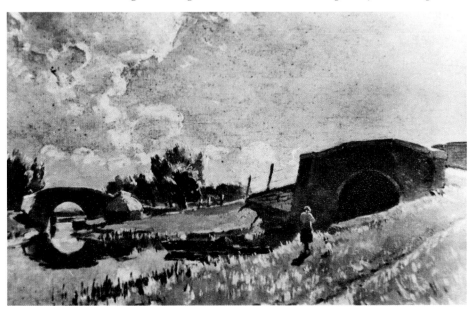

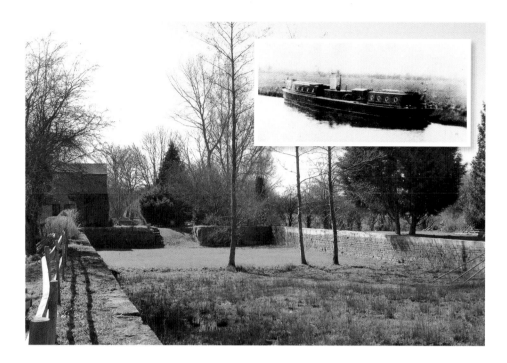

Latton Basin

The large, rectangular, stone-lined Latton Basin is now restored; its walls survive virtually intact except on the north side. Opposite was the entrance into the North Wilts Canal via a stop lock, with the lock and toll cottage alongside. In 1896, de Salis's boat *Dragonfly* lay hereabouts during his inspection tour of the canals (inset). Alfred Howse was Latton's lock-keeper; he and his wife Prudence also ran a small market garden business selling produce in Cricklade market. Here, around 1915, they are surrounded by their two sons and eight daughters.

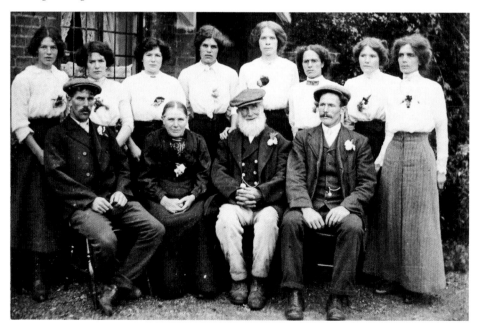

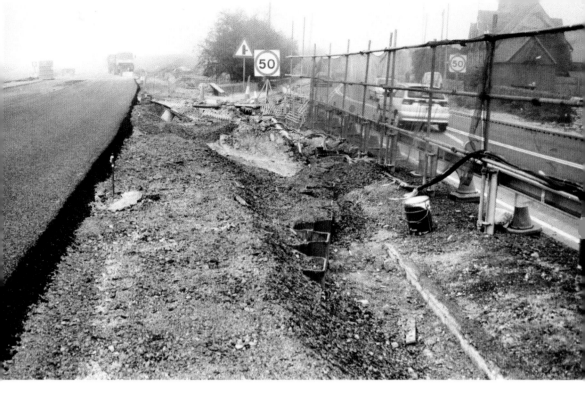

Changes at Latton

The eye of faith is required to picture the canal line where it met the old Cirencester to Swindon road; the modern A419 bypassing Latton has changed the landscape. Gone is the original Latton Bridge, the first to be demolished after closure in 1927, where the canal crossed under the road at a sharp right angle. After a ten-year battle, a culvert was inserted where new road meets old line, seen through the murk in the winter of 1997, the figures marking the line. Preserved for the future, this will turn out to be one of the great turning points in the canal's restoration. Further along, Latton Lock has vanished.

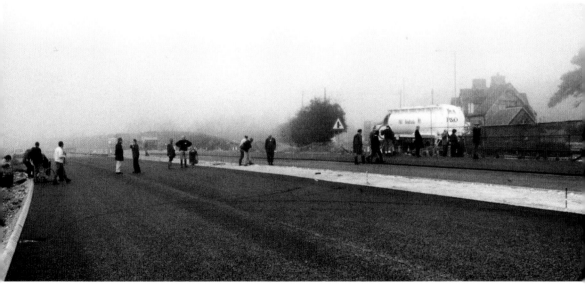

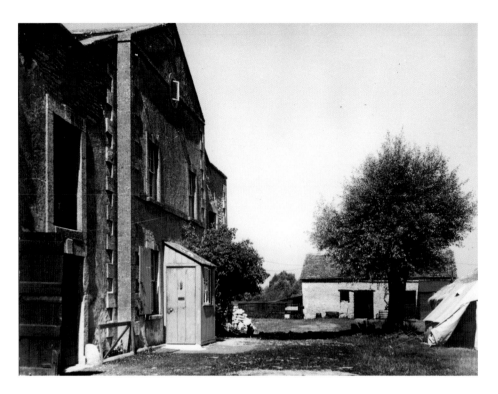

Cricklade Wharf & Wharf House

Cricklade Wharf is one of the three Thames & Severn examples of this particular design, the building functioning firstly as accommodation for the wharfinger in the central part and secondly as storage space for goods on either side and to the rear of the living accommodation, all under the one large roof. Despite alterations, the façade remains largely intact, and the rear elevation reveals the functional storage nature of the building. Humphrey Household's charming midsummer study in August 1949 is compared with the view from the rear in March 1980.

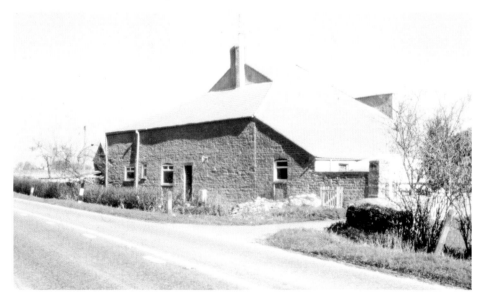

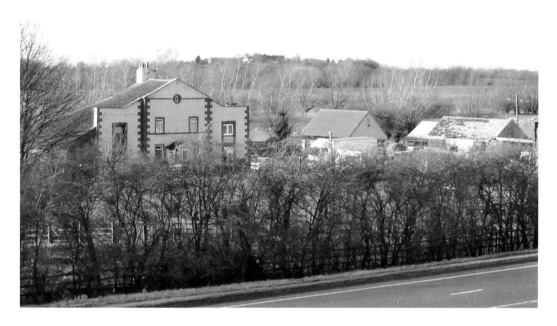

Cricklade Wharf

Wharf Farm is another example of a refurbished canal building. Reroofed, and with its façade maintained and redecorated, the building has an impact when seen from the dual carriageway. Small stables still survive, and the old diamond-shaped basin, now filled in, forms a paddock in front of the buildings. This painting from around 1920 records hayricks standing on the wharf and Fairford or Kempsford Lane Bridge beyond, now levelled and another lost feature.

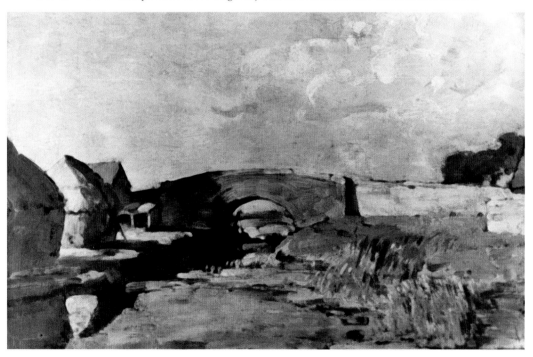

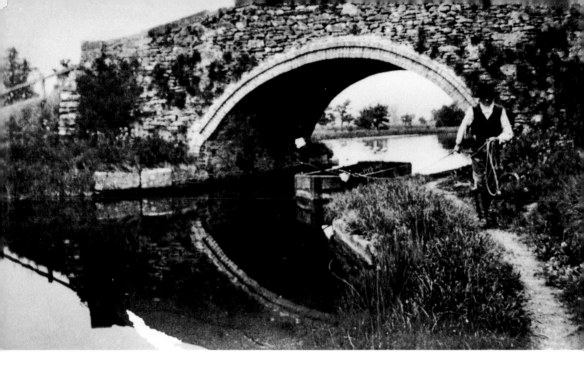

'Old Willum' at Eisey

At what is believed to be Eisey Bridge, built in stone not brick, these two images are from the writer Temple Thurston's travels when preparing his delightfully nostalgic *The Flower of Gloster*, published in 1911. They capture a rare scene of the local lengthman at work keeping the towpath clear with his small boat. Immortalised now as 'Old Willum', and a symbol of the last years in the life of the old Thames & Severn, his area of responsibility stretched from Latton to Lechlade.

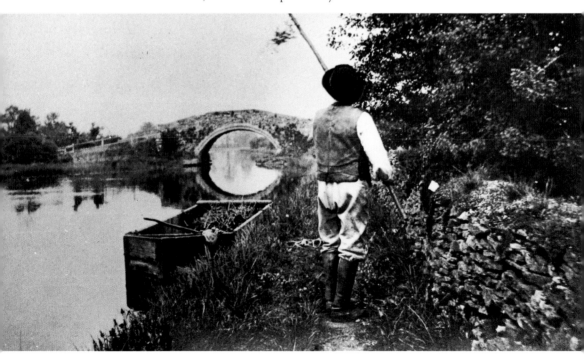

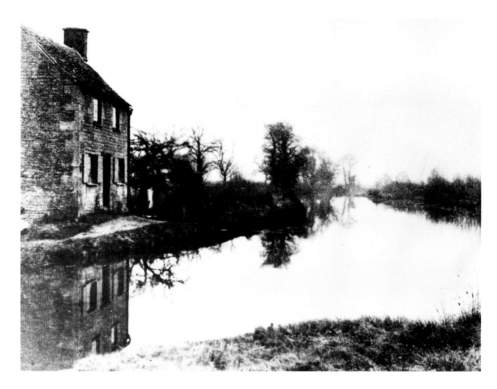

Eisey Lock & Lock Cottage

Like its twin at Wilmoreway, Eisey Cottage was isolated and reached only by boat or a walk along the towpath. Both date from 1831 and housed lengthmen redeployed along their respective lengths – the man here was moved up from Marston Meysey. In this 1896 de Salis view, the scene is one of undisturbed calm. Although the cottage remains derelict (and empty since 1969), a restoration project for Eisey Lock has progressed, seen here in May 2012.

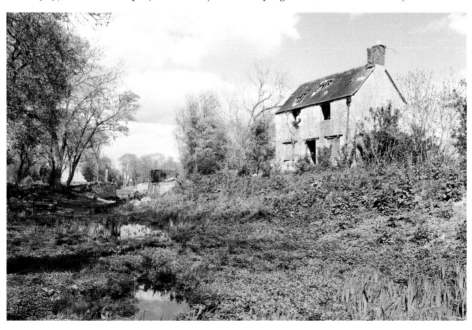

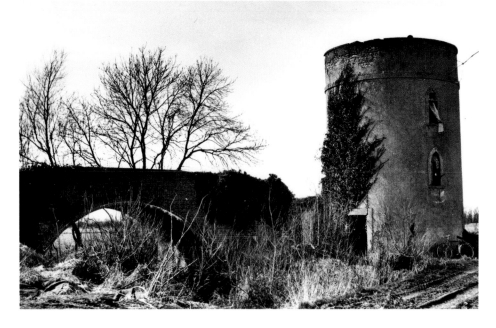

Marston Meysey Round House

In 1961 the round house stood isolated and decaying alongside its bridge. The stucco remained, and the function and design of the three-storey building exactly mirrored its companions at Coates and Inglesham. This was once a tiny country wharf, some distance from the village of Marston Meysey. Today, it is very difficult to appreciate the optimism of the canal proprietors in establishing such a remote wharf serving a wide rural area. Below, substantial rebuilding and extension, while respecting the round house's integrity, is underway in summer 1986 to create a new home once again.

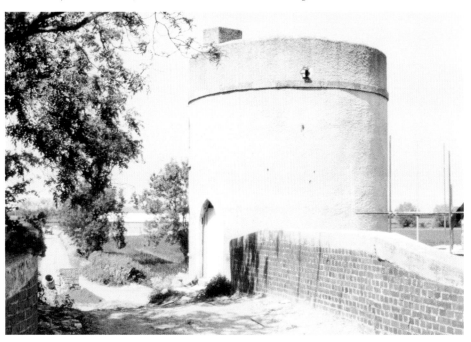

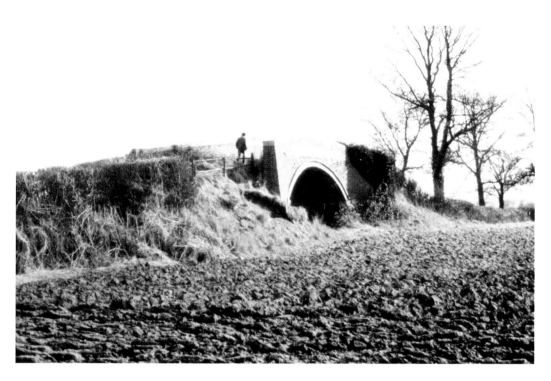

Bridges Across the Canal

Isolated, abandoned or destroyed bridges are another feature of the canal's eastern sections. Ruck's Bridge is a good example and so too is Oatlands Bridge, seen here isolated in the fields in 1972, then as now. Both exhibit the original humpback design, executed in brick. Access routes into fields or localised pedestrian routes could just as easily be served by a swing bridge, as seen here behind The Green at Kempsford, dating from 1899 and close to the River Thames.

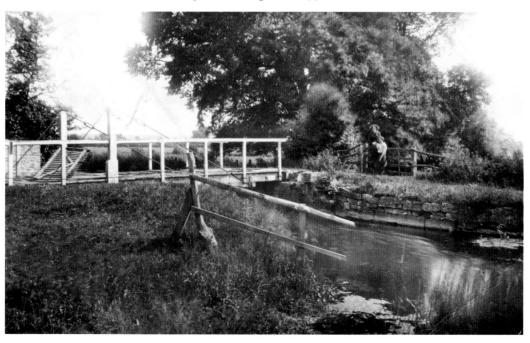

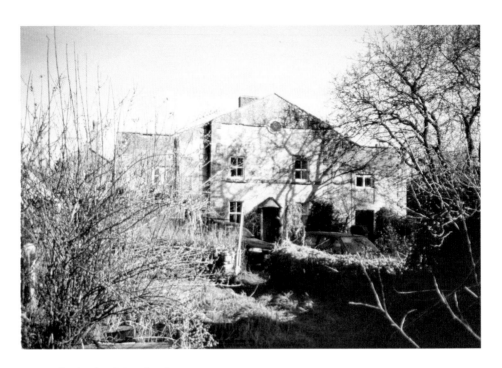

Kempsford Wharf & Wharf House

Wharf Lane is the clue to where the wharf house stands, with its back to the road, facing down to the canal. Although built to the same design and purpose as Cirencester and Cricklade, it is a narrower building. On the wharf lay what remained of the ticket office, the stables and the various cart and storage sheds. Beside the entrance, the small whitewashed cottage was the wharf's beerhouse, where drinks were served through a hatch. Gentle decay was the order of the day, until refurbishment in recent years. These views date from the winter of 1998/99.

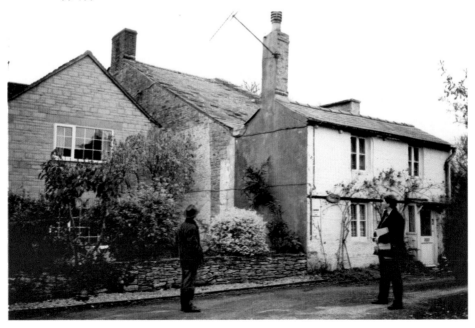

People on the Canal

Ordinary life for country people around the canal was not always well recorded by the camera. But Temple Thurston's eye and felicity with his text not only created a 'highlight of canal literature' but recorded such scenes at this: two country ladies dressed in their white bonnets and aprons coming over a humpbacked bridge, almost certainly along this eastern section. Thurston builds them into his story at Marston Meysey. The horse wears ear protectors to keep off the flies. At Inglesham, the last lock-keeper was John Rawlings, seen here on the round house steps in this group celebrating some family event. He remained at Inglesham until the canal's final days, and kept busy hiring out a fleet of boats, with his daughter selling refreshments to people boating, fishing and enjoying the river.

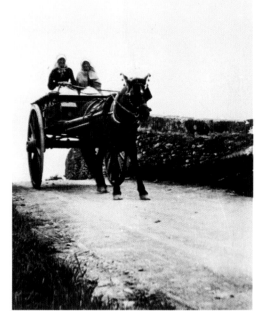

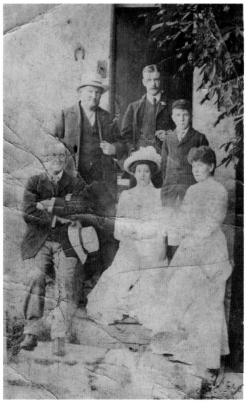

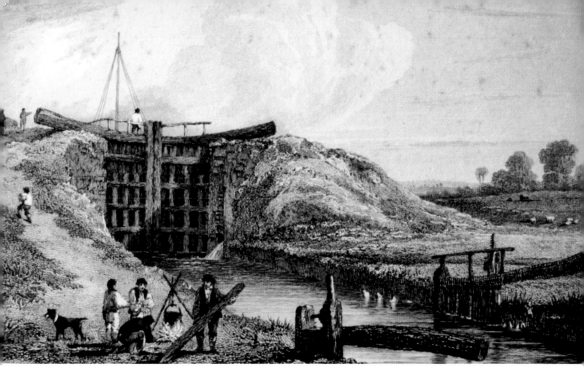

Dudgrove 'Double' Lock

This lock has an interesting story. It is the only example of its type on the canal. In W. B. Cooke's illustration of 1814 published in *The Thames 1811–22*, a barge is in the top lock. With a combined drop of 11 feet and 6 inches, the middle gates look impressively high and the lower lock mean in comparison. The 1896 de Salis image captures the same rather lonely scene. The upper chamber in typical red brick has a 9-foot fall, and leads directly into the roughly built lower chamber, constructed of loose stone walling with only a 2-foot 6-inch fall.

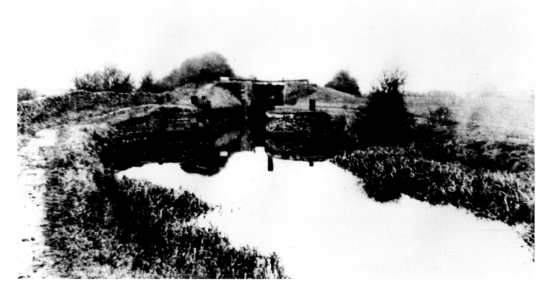

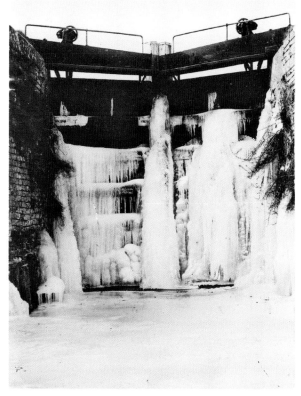

Dudgrove 'Double' Lock

The canal had been built this far by early 1789 but the final route to join the Thames had yet to be marked out on the ground or even agreed. The cause of the dispute was the state of the upper reaches of the river, a notoriously ill-kept section that was difficult for navigation. The issue was eventually resolved in favour of creating a further fall at Dudgrove, and the lower lock is the result. In the winter of 1897, the middle gates froze up dramatically. In May 2002, they were derelict but remained in position.

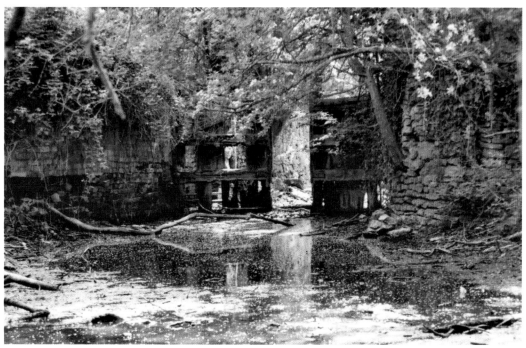

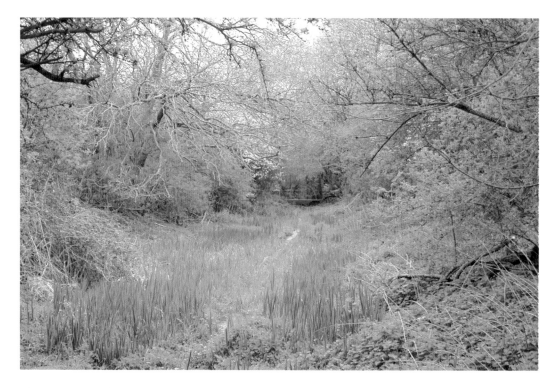

The Eastern Reaches

The 3 miles between Kempsford and Inglesham has long been isolated and the canal line even more so. The occasional bridge, such as this simple structure, was the only feature after brick bridges were dropped following closure. Until the link with the Thames is reached at Inglesham, the life of the canal and its traffic is even more remote than elsewhere, long ago replaced by other canal routes and means of transport, but the memory lingers...

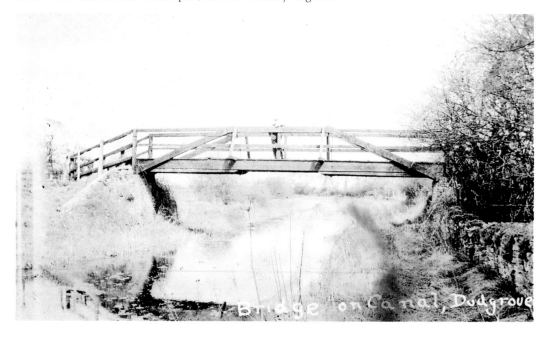

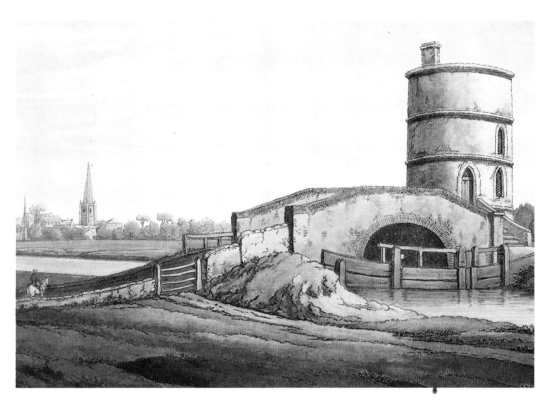

Inglesham Lock, Bridge & Round House

At Inglesham, the canal descended into the Thames, and round house, bridge and lock provide the classic Thames & Severn group. Farington's drawing, published by Boydell in June 1793, shows the canal in its very early days, with the elegant spire of Lechlade church downriver. Throughout the twentieth century, this scene formed a regular backdrop for photography. The bridge bears the date 14 November 1789, just five days before the first boat passed through the canal and into the Thames.

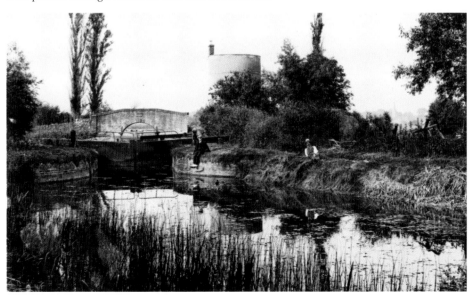

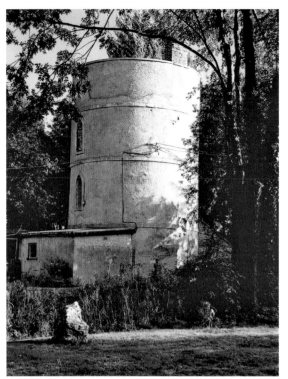

Inglesham Round House

Until 1996, the round house had one tenant for nearly fifty years and remained largely unmodernised; here again is the inverted conical roof and a fine set of steps. The scene is captured in sunshine, in September 2005 and July 2002 respectively. The terminal basin just above the lock was used as a turning pound for barges. It also serves as a reminder that, including the 1¼-mile arm to Cirencester, the total journey is some 30 miles from Stroud, which when added to the 7-plus miles of the Stroudwater completes the entire journey from Severn to Thames.

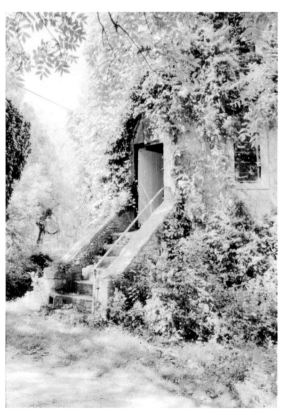

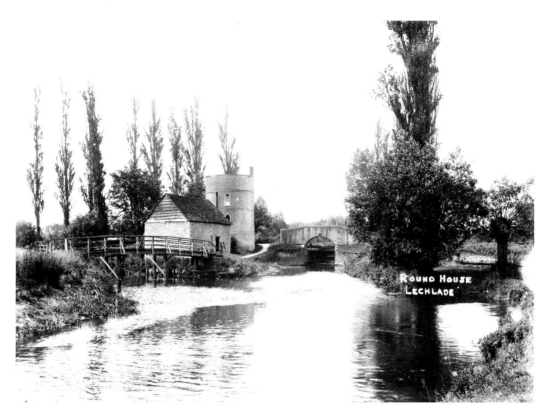

From Inglesham into the Thames

The group view is just as attractive from below, seen from the river. The warehouse alongside provided the same storage and security of goods in transit as similar buildings at other wharves along the canal. It survives as an integral part of the scene today, seen here in May 2002. In the earlier view, the upstream Thames is under the bridge to the left; the Coln comes in from the right.

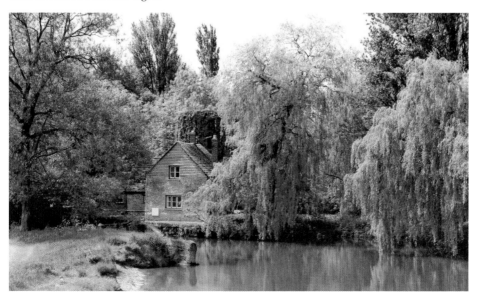

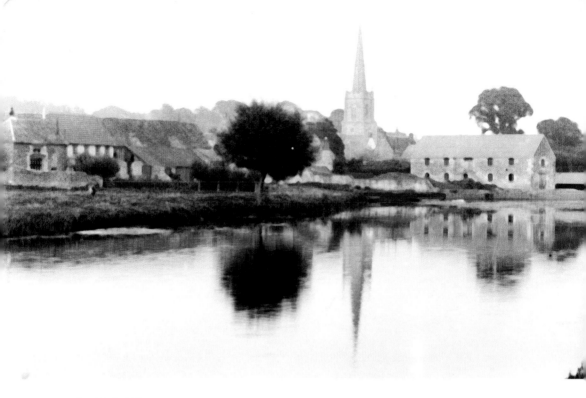

Lechlade Wharves

Today's leisure use rather disguises Lechlade's historic role as an 'inland port' with various wharves on the Thames, but these two views give something of that flavour. In 1813, the canal company removed its eastern base from cramped, isolated Inglesham by acquiring the already well-established Parkend coal wharf in Lechlade, with its fine warehouse, seen here to the right of the church. Upstream is an older, probably seventeenth-century, warehouse facing the free wharf. Below, Parkend wharf's layout is clear, with a warehouse to the right facing the building adapted for the canal company's agent.

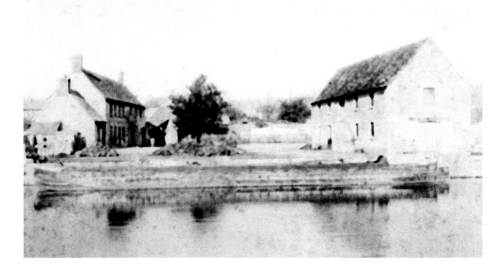

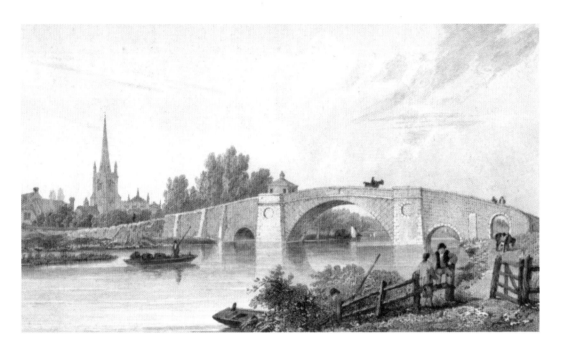

Lechlade on Thames

Halfpenny Bridge across the Thames makes a fitting finale to any tour of the Thames & Severn Canal, shown to good effect here in W. B. Cooke's engraving published in July 1815. It was close to the canal, built in 1793 for the turnpike road between Banbury, Burford and Highworth. This added to Lechlade's value as a gathering point for river traffic. The graceful central arch remains an attractive feature of the river scene along with the tiny toll-house on the downstream side, a rare survivor today and not used as such since 1839.

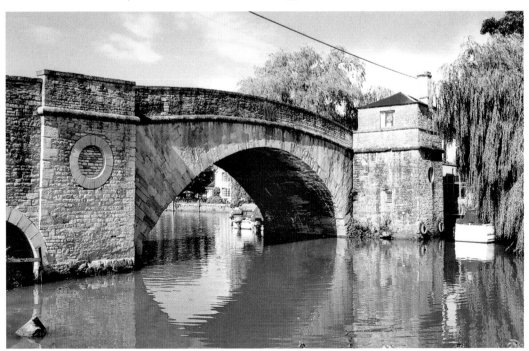

Acknowledgements

An interest stretching back nearly half a century inevitably owes much to the many kindnesses of a great number of people, valuable as sources of information, photographs and other records of the Thames & Severn Canal, from its working life and during its long period of dereliction as well as the restoration revival years since the early 1970s. There are too many to thank individually in fact, but the following are particularly acknowledged for their help with this volume, providing access to their own collections or allowing use of their own material, for which the author is as ever especially grateful: Howard Beard (Stroud), Edwin Cuss, Philip Griffiths and Rick Martin (all Cirencester), Mike Mills (Chalford Hill), David McDougall (Taynton), John Loosley and the Oakridge History Group, John Espley for his archive of the early restoration years, and Hugh McKnight and Michael Ware for access many years ago to the de Salis and Temple Thurston archives respectively. A more contemporary archive is the one Nick Bird is creating via his Cotswold Canals in Pictures website. Thanks to Cotswold Canals Trust, especially Ken Burgin, Chief Executive; David Jowett, editor of the immensely valuable *The Trow*; John Maxted; and to Stroud District Council where David Marshall, Canal Partnership Manager, and Jon Pontefract kindly provided recent images and updates. Lechlade Historical Society once again gave access to its record of the canal's eastern section. All other material is from the author's own collection.

Although not all images can be acknowledged to their original photographer (often appearing as postcards, of course), some familiar local names and studios stand out, including W. Dennis Moss of Cirencester, F. Major of Bisley, F. Colville of Chalford and of course H. W. Taunt of Oxford, who had a particular interest in the River Thames. Later photographers recording the canal scene, often by walking its length, include Frank Lloyd (Gloucester) and Harry Townley (Rodborough), and as ever the resources and support from the Corinium Museum in Cirencester and Gloucestershire Archives are duly acknowledged with thanks.

Websites

www.cotswoldcanals.com (Cotswold Canals Trust)
www.cotswoldcanalsproject.org (Cotswold Canals Partnership)
www.stroudwater.co.uk (Company of Proprietors of the Stroudwater Navigation)
www.cotswoldcanals.net (Cotswold Canals in Pictures)
www.cotswoldcanalsheritage.org.uk

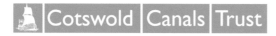